Essays on *The Glass Menagerie*

This volume traces the growth of Tennessee Williams from being a fragile child to becoming one of America's greatest playwrights, also highlighting the playwright's deep indebtedness to Southern literary conventions. The book analyses Williams's wonderful play with the sense of time and shows how in *The Glass Menagerie*, as in all memory plays, the protagonist ruminates over the past, re-evaluates himself in that context, and has a deeper understanding of the present, eventually using memory to recover from past trauma. One of the chapters analyses the use of the new form in *Menagerie* that Williams and his contemporaries had begun experimenting with, what Williams referred to as 'plastic theatre.' Twentieth-century American poetic drama turned out to be contemporary, seeking the universal emotional and psychic truths and simultaneously portraying American life and culture with authenticity. The book also involves an in-depth study of the characters in *Menagerie*. Tom Wingfield has been critiqued in relationship to the absent father, the formidable mother, and the soulmate sister; and the author has focused on, amongst many things, the gender issue. She has provided an analysis and critique of the reproduction of sex and gender and has brought the reader's attention to Tom's and the playwright's own struggle to strike a balance between the masculine and the feminine.

Tania Chakravertty is the Dean of Students' Welfare, Diamond Harbour Women's University, West Bengal, India. She is the author of *Ernest Hemingway and the Fluidity of Gender: A Socio-Cultural Analysis of Selected Works*.

Routledge Focus on Literature

Creative Writing and the Experiences of Others
Strategies for Outsiders
Nandita Dinesh

Emotionality
Heterosexual Love and Emotional Development in Popular Romance
Arvanitaki Eirini

Digital Culture and the Hermeneutic Tradition
Suspicion, Trust, and Dialogue
Inge van de Ven and Lucie Chateau

Dreams in Chinese Fiction
Spiritism, Aestheticism, and Nationalism
Johannes D. Kaminski

Remapping Energopolitics
Blue Humanities, Geophilosophy and Sri Lankan Minor Writings
Abhisek Ghosal

Colonial Philippines in Italian Travel Writing
"Italians" Interpreting Difference
Jillian Loise Melchor

Essays on *The Glass Menagerie*
Truth in the Pleasant Disguise of Illusion
Tania Chakravertty

For more information about this series, please visit www.routledge.com/Routledge-Focus-on-Literature/book-series/RFLT

Essays on *The Glass Menagerie*

Truth in the Pleasant Disguise of Illusion

Tania Chakravertty

NEW YORK AND LONDON

First published 2025
by Routledge
605 Third Avenue, New York, NY 10158

and by Routledge
4 Park Square, Milton Park, Abingdon, Oxon, OX14 4RN

Routledge is an imprint of the Taylor & Francis Group, an informa business

ISBN: 978-1-032-81307-3 (hbk)
ISBN: 978-1-032-82387-4 (pbk)
ISBN: 978-1-003-50424-5 (ebk)

DOI: 10.4324/9781003504245

Typeset in Times New Roman
by SPi Technologies India Pvt Ltd (Straive)

Dedicated to my mother, Shampa Chakravertty (who does not resemble Amanda Wingfield in the least). I am grateful to her for the constant inspiration and support she has given me throughout my life.

Contents

Introduction

Chapter 1 involves biographical information regarding the playwright Tennessee Williams (born Thomas Lanier Williams), tracing his growth from being a fragile child reared in the home of his grandfather to becoming one of America's greatest playwrights. I have carefully critiqued his relationship with his father, a rowdy and boisterous individual and a traveling salesman, and that with his mother, a Southern belle who enjoyed the affluence and status of her father, a liberal and progressive individual. Tom was immensely close to his sister Rose. With a grandmother and a mother both of whom were artists, and a sister as his close companion, Thomas turned out to be a child sensitive towards girls and women. The biographical study also scrutinises the greatest shock that came with the move his family made as his father accepted a managerial position in The International Shoe Company in St. Louis and moved the entire family to an unsightly tenement building in St. Louis, Missouri, a move that destroyed the carefree and idyllic nature of his boyhood.

I have analysed his university years and his slow move towards commercial success. After finishing high school, in 1929, Tennessee Williams enrolled at the University of Missouri to study journalism. He went to the university for three years and also got involved with the Reserve Officers Training Corps (ROTC). However, his grades were poor, and he failed the ROTC. After his third year, his father got him a position in the International Shoe Company factory, and he worked there for two years. He hated this position and found solace in creativity—writing poems and stories after work at night. Eventually, depression took its toll, and Williams suffered a nervous breakdown. He went to Memphis, Tennessee, to recuperate with his grandfather, who had moved there after retirement. After recuperating, Williams returned to St. Louis, where he connected with several poets studying at Washington University. He continued writing and had some of his earlier works produced. In 1937, he returned to college, enrolling at the University of Iowa, from where he graduated the following year. It was the University of Iowa that shaped his career as a playwright.

DOI: 10.4324/9781003504245-1

After leaving Iowa, he drifted around the country, picking up odd jobs and collecting experiences. After this came a brief venture in Hollywood that did not work out. Williams had written a short story titled "Portrait of a Girl in Glass", which he turned into a screenplay titled *The Gentleman Caller*; Williams offered MGM the draft, which was turned down. He, however, claimed that it would last longer than *Gone with the Wind*. Williams's words eventually turned out to be prophetic. Thought of as Williams's first major play, *The Glass Menagerie* was to become one of the greatest American plays, one of the most anthologised, most performed, and most translated of all American plays.

In order to best understand Tennessee Williams and his most celebrated play *The Glass Menagerie*, I have analysed and critiqued the context(s) which led him to write experimental plays, including *Menagerie*.

Chapter 2 is a study of autobiographical elements in *Menagerie*. Tennessee Williams was named Thomas Lanier Williams by his parents at birth, and his nickname had been Tom. This awareness instantly alerts the reader to the possibility that Tom Wingfield is a depiction of Tennessee Williams and that *Menagerie* is an autobiographical play. Williams remarked once that if it were true that all of his works were autobiographical, it was equally true that none of his works was. Though the play drew much from personal experiences, the events of the play are not merely depictions of anyone's personal history.

The first thing that he drew from life and transformed was the Williams apartment on Enright Avenue in St Louis, Missouri. Mr. Wingfield senior, in *Menagerie*, is shown to have abandoned his family years back. In real life, however, Cornelius Williams had left his job with the telephone company and had taken up another with the International Shoe Company in St. Louis. His father coerced him to join the shoe company during his first stint of university education. Williams later classified this time as the most miserable two years of his life. The wage-earning experience took a toll on his mental health just as it does to Tom. He put much of himself in Tom Wingfield, loathing his clerical job and squirming to escape.

Among the many things that Williams drew from personal experiences, the most distressing were his interactions with his mother Edwina Dakin Williams. Edwina incessantly kept on reminiscing about her life and the experiences in her youth in the Deep South. Dakin family accounts show that Edwina on one occasion received thirty gentlemen callers in a single day. Edwina Dakin, just like Amanda Wingfield, committed the mistake of falling in love with the wrong man and choosing the wrong man as her husband amongst her many gentlemen callers.

The prototype for Laura was Williams's sister Rose. Williams's attachment to Rose was tremendous; the siblings, only sixteen months apart, were as inseparable as twins. The child Tennessee was quiet and observant, and Rose was lively and spirited. Rose, like Laura, loved playing old records on the Victrola record player and often taught her brother the dance steps she knew. Like Laura, she too had enrolled in the Rubicam's Business College to learn typing and shorthand but, unable to cope with the pressure, had quit abruptly. And just like Laura in the play, she kept this a secret from their mother, wandered about in the city, and returned home late in the afternoons with the pretence of having attended her classes. Rose, sprightly and vivacious, had no trouble, however, attracting men in her teens and early twenties. In early youth, far from being shy and demure like Laura, she was much like the extrovert and talkative mother Amanda. Another important event drawn from life was the event of arranging a gentleman caller for Rose by her brother Tom. At their mother's insistence, Williams invited Jim Connor to dinner only to discover that, just like Jim O'Connor in *Menagerie*, he was already engaged.

Chapter 3 is a study of Williams's deep indebtedness to Southern literary conventions. Williams was drawn to the splendour of the Old South and took pride in his own 'aristocratic' connections. The playwright had a continuing love/hate relationship with the culture he was born into, and his criticisms of the South are often harsh. As a realist, he decided not to depict the Southern elite idealistically, as Margaret Mitchell had done. Most of Williams's plays reflected binaries which were praised or satirized in Southern writing. Williams portrayed the charm of Southern culture yet deconstructed it in play after play.

In most of his plays, the personal dilemmas of individuals and social predicaments are inextricably linked with the South. Williams manifests a belief in the metaphorical importance of the South, viewing it as a doomed civilisation yet carrying the elegance and legacy of the past. None of Williams's characters escapes the burdens of his/her personal and regional histories.

Williams's male protagonists do not fit into the constructs of the stereotypical Southern hero. Williams did not abandon the concept of the hero but adapted it to fit the hero into a world which was hopelessly corrupt, violent, and unjust.

Menagerie would fall under the Piedmont category from amongst the three regions—Tidewater, Piedmont, and the 'deep' South. Small-town Southern life with its class segregation was part of the Piedmont tradition. Amanda Wingfield is a fine example of the conservative patriarchal feudalistic South. In *Menagerie*, as in the other plays, the Southern aristocrats are challenged, sometimes by upstarts of Anglo-Saxon descent and also by other newcomers who bear Italian, Polish, or Jewish names.

The exquisite poetic qualities in Williams's language come from his Southern origin. *Menagerie* is full of exquisitely poetic passages.

In Chapter 4, I have dealt with the playwright's wonderful play with the sense of time. As Tom declares, the play's actions are set in the 1930s, but once the spectators begin to accustom themselves to that era, they are taken back, through Amanda, to a time even more remote. Yet this play is not a typical memory play associated with the protagonist reminiscing over the past. The play also expresses the present that Tom inhabits. The remote past motivates the characters, and the closer past constitutes the play's action. Williams's manifestation of the past in *Menagerie* is varied, involving individual memories. As Tom says that he will be presenting "truth in the pleasant disguise of illusion", the personal past and the accompanying *angst* (his own and theirs) become universal. Eventually, all the three characters—Amanda, Tom, and Laura Wingfield—fail in their attempts to escape and break their bonds with time. The mother, Amanda, keeps yearning for the past and remains emotionally tied to the past. Tom eagerly looks towards the future. For Tom, the future holds the promise of escape from the unbearable present, made all the more unbearable because of Amanda's recollection of the past. Sadly, Tom's plan for the future is accomplished with his abandonment of both the past and the present. For Laura, neither past, nor present, nor future connects her to the real world, and she remains imprisoned in the static present.

In memory plays, characters mull over moments from the past, re-evaluate themselves in that context, and simultaneously form a deeper understanding of the present. In some cases, faced with crisis, playwrights and the actors may use memory plays to recover from past trauma. In *Menagerie*, Tom Wingfield introduces the audience to his family memories, thereby living in two time zones, re-living moments from the past and simultaneously existing in the present in front of the spectators. We do not really see Tom's mother and sister, but we see his memory of them. The depictions are filtered through Tom's perception. He speaks fondly of his sister, shows mixed feelings towards his mother, and also remembers not just their lives and the gentleman caller but also another member of the family—his father—the absent father whose memory hurts them very much. In the theatric retelling, Tom as actor and narrator looks back and contextualises the traumatic events in his past life. Eventually, he escapes, having used creative expression which becomes therapeutic; the objectivity and detachment of Tom the artist exorcise the pain as he creates the play.

In Chapter 5, I have analysed the use of a new form in *Menagerie*, what Williams referred to as 'plastic theatre'. Williams and his contemporaries began experimenting with new forms as opposed to the traditional Aristotelian ones, leading to the creation of an anti-classical form. Twentieth-century American poetic drama, as practised by Eugene O'Neill and Tennessee Williams, turned out to be contemporary, maintaining full contact with reality and simultaneously seeking the core essential emotional and psychic truths. In the "Author's Production Notes" to *Menagerie*, Williams mentions that he is attempting to indulge in this new form of poetic drama. To Williams, conventional American realistic theatre was dull and humdrum, and he wished to create a new kind of poetry on stage. Williams's poetic drama and its form turned out to be distinctly American, portraying the authenticity of American life and culture.

The first thing that strikes us as we watch *Menagerie* is its simplicity. Keeping this simplicity intact, Williams presented the play as a series of episodes instead of adhering to the traditional three-act or five-act structure. *Menagerie* eventually evolved as a play with seven scenes.

The playwright defined *The Glass Menagerie* as well as *Camino Real* and *American Blues* as plays of 'personal lyricism,' suggesting that his plays were vehicles of the expression of the self. There are similarities with Japanese Noh-drama, in which the story unfolds through remembered fragments of experience. And as Williams had emphasised in his production notes, the lighting and music were not mere accompaniments but were integral parts of his play.

Of all the stage devices that Williams used successfully, a prime one was the use of scrims/gauze scenery. Williams made an exhaustive use of gauze scenery in *Menagerie*; scenes behind the gauze appeared and dissolved, just as memories appear and dissolve in one's mind. Williams also made use of the screen with 'legends' or title cards like those in silent films. Williams's use of magic lanterns was also remarkable. The magic lanterns or the slide projections produced hazy, flexible, and plastic images. The series of titles and hazy unfixed images manifest the playwright's attempt to portray the fuzzy and nebulous world of dreams.

Amongst all American playwrights, it was Williams who learnt much from cinema and cinematic techniques, and *Menagerie*, amongst all his plays, is the most cinematic in form. In his comments on lighting and in his use of the same in the play, Williams frequently suggested cinematic camera shots. There were techniques that Williams adopted from the cinema—long shot, montage, the shot/reverse shot leading to the suture, and the patriarchal gaze.

Chapter 6 is a study of the characters in *The Glass Menagerie*. In one's study of the characters in *Menagerie*, one might begin by asking how many characters the play presents us with. One could say there are the Wingfields and Jim O'Connor, the gentleman caller; one could also say that there is only one character in the play: Tom Wingfield. Though Amanda is a formidable character, and though the glass menagerie belongs to Laura, the play belongs to Tom. Tom opens the play and also closes it; Amanda, Laura, and the gentleman caller do appear in the play, but the audience sees not the characters but Tom's memory of them. In *Menagerie*, each character is troubled, lonely, frustrated, and desperate.

In *Menagerie*, the absent father is central to the dramatic action but does not ever appear on the stage. In plays, absent characters often exist in a past time, namely a time prior to the action of the play; they may exist in the present time but are spatially removed from the action of the play.

Absent characters are often represented by iconic markers as photographs or metonymic signs as in *Menagerie*. Like some of his other plays, *Menagerie* portrays an absent father who remains an imposing figure even after he has left. The absent father Mr. Wingfield, who abandoned his family years back, is not given a first name in the play. He is shown to be a solipsistic individual and a fugitive. Amanda idolizes him, and Tom transforms him into a quasi-mythical figure.

I have critiqued the relationship between Amanda and Tom Wingfield, relying much on the theories stated in *The Reproduction of Mothering* by Nancy Chodorow. Clearly based on his mother, Edwina Dakin Williams, Amanda Wingfield has been portrayed by Williams as a complex human being—a formidable character, a domineering mother. Amanda Wingfield fits in with the ideology of the 'moral mother' which Chodorow rightly opines was produced during the early capitalist period in America. Her attentions and moral guidance get focussed entirely around her children, a situation which leads to violent clashes with her son. Amanda eagerly wants people, especially her children, to listen to her—to her memories, which contain facts albeit seen through rose-coloured lenses. She keeps on digging into her strata of memories, which her children are forced to listen to. She refuses to accept the present and, what is worse, refuses to accept what is true, and that includes her daughter's lameness. Unfortunately, Amanda Wingfield fails to extricate herself from the past and associate herself with the present and fails also to comprehend how much of a misfit her children will be in the present times if they model themselves after her and follow her instructions. It is not Tom but Amanda who is a true romantic, a person obsessed with the past and a person remote from the present realities.

Tom Wingfield is a character no less complex as compared with his mother. The audience sees the entire action of *Menagerie* filtered through the consciousness of Tom, the narrator. Images of entrapment abound in *Menagerie*, and the protagonist manifests a desire for freedom right from the beginning, right from the time the memory begins to unfold. One reason why Tom Wingfield wishes to escape is because Tom and Laura are victims of their mother's domination. Instead of indulging in his mother's romantic entrapment in the past, and determined not to let her spoil his life completely, Tom seeks adventure, reality, and freedom from this female-dominant but father-absent family. For Tom Wingfield, the home becomes a trap from which he must escape to achieve a sense of selfhood and a masculine identity. In patriarchal cultures, masculine identification is predominantly a gender role identification in stark contrast to feminine identification, which is predominantly *parental*. In the absence of her husband, Amanda expects her son to take up the patriarchal 'masculine' roles of provider and protector. Tom, identifying himself with his father, thinks of himself as a failure, in social and economic terms, in the masculine roles he needs to play. In spite of all that Amanda does for her children and in spite of her overprotective concern, Tom identifies with his father and chooses to turn away from his well-meaning mother. Though he is called Shakespeare by Jim, Tom is not really a poet. He is not a romantic either. Coupled with his rebellious act in the warehouse comes rebellion against his domineering yet romantic mother. His escape is also not the quick impulsive act of the romantic poet but one which is deliberately planned. He eventually exercises his freedom and proves his manhood by abandoning his mother and sister. This running away ironically makes him a man in traditional patriarchal terms. However, though he disentangles himself from the domestic ties and the feminine, he simultaneously fails to conform to the rugged masculine culture he has run to. Tom fails to leave behind the feminine part of himself. A failure he may be, in traditional, social, patriarchal terms, yet Tom succeeds in evading the rigid categories of gender.

It is interesting to note that the origins of the play lie in a short story "Portrait of a Girl in Glass," which Williams wrote in 1941. Laura, the painfully shy girl in *Menagerie*, is constantly associated with glass. Indeed, hers is also a portrait of a girl in glass. Laura Wingfield manifests a social ineptitude; she lacks the social intelligence to understand the need for preparing herself to earn a living. Goaded by Amanda, she joins the Rubicam's Business School to learn typing and shorthand but eventually drops out after a nervous breakdown. Her social ineptitude makes her take refuge in her glass collection, the eponymous glass menagerie, and her father's old phonograph records. Children of absent fathers are often 'lost children,' failures, alienated from themselves and the world that surrounds them. The menagerie traps Laura with its pristine beauty and austerity as she finds contentment in the world of her glass animals; she also refrains from seeking happiness from the outside world. She surrenders to the unchanging world of her glass animals, wishing to escape from the mundane everyday world and the world of the present into a world of fantasy and delusion bereft of her lameness—a defect she is painfully aware of no matter how much her mother tries to hide it with euphemisms. It is entirely Amanda's decision to get Laura a husband so that she can evade being like other spinsters. In stark contrast to her mother, Laura emerges as a woman who resists the male gaze in *Menagerie* and comes to represent an alternative to the ones complying with the conventional role of woman in a patriarchal society. Contrary to what her mother wanted, Jim's conversations and encouragement expose her vulnerability like never before, and she is eventually shattered one more time. She knows that she must again escape to her father's old phonograph records and her little glass animals.

The audience/reader is made to understand that after his graduation, the young gentleman caller, Jim O'Connor, the high school hero for both the siblings, has failed to fulfil the promise of his high school years. The young gentleman who showed so much of potential has turned out to be no better than Tom Wingfield, working as a clerk in a shoe warehouse. Jim speaks of his plans of enrolling in a night school course where he would take up radio engineering and public speaking, and he epitomises the American dream of success, glorified in the romances of Horatio Alger. This ambition endears Jim to Amanda. Jim shows the promise of becoming the mythical American 'self-made man.' He arrives as an "emissary from the world of reality" and may be called the chief spokesman for the American dream. To Jim, the warehouse, instead of being a prison, as it is to Tom, becomes a rung in the ladder towards future success. In spite of his confidence, there remains an apprehension that Jim is also harbouring illusions, just like the Wingfields. Jim's ordinariness is shown in the play through the unicorn/horse symbolism. Without its horn, it becomes just an ordinary horse without the aura of distinctiveness.

Chapter 7 is the concluding chapter. This year marks the 80th year of the first production and performance of *The Glass Menagerie*, and this book *Essays on The Glass Menagerie: Truth in the Pleasant Disguise of Illusion* celebrates that. The play's success story began on 26 December 1944, and since 1945 the play has been performed constantly by community theatres and playhouses and by major companies, and it continues to be one of the most frequently revived of all American plays. I have furnished an account and briefly described some of the revivals of *The Glass Menagerie* in Broadway and other theatres. I have tried also to analyse why, even after eighty years, *The Glass Menagerie* continues to mesmerise audiences worldwide.

1 Tennessee Williams

The Formative Years

The second of Cornelius and Edwina Williams's three children, Tennessee Williams was born Thomas Lanier Williams on 26 March 1911 in Columbus, Mississippi. His father was a traveling salesman, and because his father was often away from home, he lived the first ten years of his life in his maternal grandparents' home. Cornelius Williams was a rowdy and boisterous individual in love with his work. Allean Hale notes that his father appeared "only often enough to upset the tranquil household and frighten his children" (11). Williams was therefore raised and reared predominantly by his mother and his grandfather, an Episcopal rector, Reverend Walter Dakin, a liberal and progressive individual. Thomas Williams, as a child, was rather delicate, plagued with several serious childhood diseases. When he was five, Tom was afflicted with diphtheria, a disease that became life-threatening. As an after-effect, he became temporarily paralysed and did not regain the full use of his legs for about two years. This made it impossible for him to attend regular school; so he read profusely in his grandfather's library and basked in music, which was so much a part of the Dakin household. His mother Edwina, possessing the beauty and finesse of a Southern belle, was shy and quiet and had a tremendous attachment to her children. She was a woman who enjoyed the affluence and status of her father. Edwina's mother was a music teacher, and Edwina herself used to perform as a singer. Tom was immensely close to his sister Rose. With a grandmother and a mother both of whom were artists, and a sister as his close companion, Thomas turned out to be a child who was sensitive towards girls and women. As Hale rightly points out, "Growing up in this female dominated environment doubtless gave Tom the empathy shown in the woman characters created by the playwright Tennessee" (11).

His childhood in Mississippi was pleasant and happy. The greatest shock to Williams came with the move his family made when he was about twelve. Life for him changed drastically as his father accepted a

DOI: 10.4324/9781003504245-2

managerial position in The International Shoe Company in St. Louis and moved the entire family to an unsightly tenement building in St. Louis. The carefree and idyllic nature of his boyhood was lost in his new urban home. It seemed that in this new city, in sharp contrast to the cultured atmosphere he had grown accustomed to, people cared only about money. Their cramped apartment and the ugliness of life in the new city made him miserable. His father, hitherto the travelling salesman, was suddenly at home most of the time, and so the home also became a tense place to live in. Edwina, suddenly feeling small, began holding back affection from her children, and Cornelius, in spite of his handsome salary, began to hold back money. Williams wrote years later that his parents were in a 'wrong marriage'.

It was in St. Louis that Rose began to distance herself from her brother, and she started to behave strangely from the time she was a teenager. His father had begun to call his sensitive and delicate son 'Miss Nancy'. In school, some of his classmates began ridiculing Thomas for his southern accent, and he began to feel like an outsider. His mother Edwina found in Thomas a confidant and, understanding her son's feeling of entrapment, bought him a second-hand typewriter. The sensitive and lonely Thomas began to write on this typewriter.

His first published story, "Isolated," appeared in *The Junior Life* when he was thirteen. In the ninth grade, he wrote a protest article titled "Demon Smoke" in the June 1925 yearbook. At sixteen, his smart answer to the question, "Can a Good Wife Be a Good Sport?" appeared in the *Smart Set* magazine, fetching him five dollars as prize money. When he was seventeen, *Weird Tales* paid him thirty-five dollars for a horror story. Since writing was fetching him money, Thomas decided that he would study journalism.

In 1929, after finishing high school, Thomas Williams enrolled at the University of Missouri to study journalism. Though the university had one of the best schools of journalism in the entire country, he found the classes unattractive. He continued to write, though, and found himself gradually drawn to alcohol. Hale reports that the university "then had a series of contests in Poetry, Essay, Story and Playwriting, each with the magnificent prize of fifty dollars" (14), adding that Thomas entered all of them. The drama contest had an incentive, the winners would have their plays produced by the Missouri Workshop. Thomas wrote his first play, *Beauty is the Word*; he did not win but received mention, the first mention ever for a freshman. This was a play where the protagonist rebels against his religious upbringing. This was followed by *Hot Milk at Three in the Morning* written in his sophomore year, where the protagonist severs ties with family. Hale mentions that this was "kitchen sink" drama, a genre popularised by John Osborne three and a half decades later.

He attended the University of Missouri for three years and also got involved with the Reserve Officers Training Corps (ROTC). However, his grades were poor, and he failed the military training in the Reserve Officers' Training Corps (ROTC). Cornelius Williams got Thomas a job in the International Shoe Company factory, a job that earned him sixty-five dollars a month. It was a "nine-to-five blue-collar world" (Hale 15) where he had to dust shoes and type numbers into a mimeograph throughout the day. He detested this position and found solace in creativity—writing poems and stories after work at night. In fact, he set a schedule of writing one story every week. Eventually, after two years, depression took its toll, and Williams suffered a nervous breakdown which gave him the much-needed release from this job.

He began to recuperate under the supervision of his grandparents, who had moved to Memphis, Tennessee, after Mr. Dakin's retirement. Here he came into contact with an amateur theatre group and wrote a play titled *Cairo! Shanghai! Bombay!* This play dealt with two sailors on leave. After his recuperation, Williams returned to St. Louis and began attending Washington University, with his grandmother sponsoring the university fees and funds. Here he met Clark Mills McBurney, French scholar and poet, who introduced him to the works of Rilke, Rimbaud, and Hart Crane and to the Union of St. Louis Artists and Writers. Mills also published twenty of Thomas's poems in the university literary paper, *The Eliot*. At Washington University, Williams also came in contact with Professor William G. B. Carson, who had a playwriting class and an amateur group called the Mummers with William Holland as director. Williams later wrote that the Mummers never put on a show that "didn't deliver a punch" (Quoted in Hale 16). For the Mummers, he wrote *Candles to the Sun*, a play about coal miners, and *Fugitive Kind*, set in a men's flophouse. *Fugitive Kind* was a failure, but he reserved the title for the future. Professor Carson's class ended every year with a one-act play contest. Williams submitted a play titled *Me, Vashya!*, which dealt with a maker and supplier of munitions set in the times of war, and he lost to a writer who submitted a light comedy. Williams soon left Washington University.

In 1937, he enrolled at the University of Iowa to study playwriting, and he graduated the following year. Hale mentions that the university:

> had just constructed a splendid Dramatic Arts building with the latest staging facilities—'the theatre is the most completely equipped in the world,' Tom wrote his mother. One of the first college radio stations, WSUI, was at Iowa, the future famous Writers' Workshop was forming, there was a literary magazine, *American Prefaces*. … Professor E. C. Mabie, who headed the Department of Dramatic Art, was forging new concepts in theatre education.
>
> (18)

Mabie taught playwriting, yet he emphasised that all students must acquire acting skills and a practical knowledge of stagecraft. As Peter Davison emphasises, "throughout the twentieth century, the writing and study of drama, the training of actors, and instruction in all aspects of the performing arts have been vigorously encouraged by universities, foundations, and local communities to a degree far beyond that prevailing in Britain" (553). Williams took a Modern Drama reading course too. The students had to submit a short play every week, and the three best plays would get produced. His emphasis on social drama led to his association with the Living Newspaper productions. Williams also studied under Professor Conkle, who was then basking in the success of his Broadway production *Prologue to Glory*. From 1937 onwards, Rose's condition had worsened. She had to be confined at the Farmington State Hospital for insanity. In 1939, Thomas Williams, frustrated and enraged because of their failure to cure his sister, wrote a play targeting physicians, and Mabie tore up this script. Thomas Williams's Living Newspaper productions at Iowa included *The Big Scene*, dealing with a Hollywood producer, and *Quit Eating*, a prison play. At the end of the session, Williams wrote *Spring Storm*, set in the South. It was the University of Iowa that shaped his career as a playwright.

Williams left Iowa, and back home he wrote *Not About Nightingales*, another prison play where he used the cinematic technique, where the thematic titles were flashed on the screen. In 1939, unable to stand his home yet again, he moved to New Orleans, trying for a Works Progress Administration job, and took a new name too—Tennessee—given some years back by his schoolmates because of his Southern accent. He sent four one-act plays and two long plays as an anthology titled *American Blues* for a Group Theatre writing contest and signed his name as Tennessee Williams. He kept on drifting around the country, picking up odd jobs. As Desmond Reid says, "[a]s clerk, lift-boy, telephone operator, waiter and cinema worker, he learned to observe people and to write about them" (431). In Hollywood, he had a brief stint as a shoe salesman. Around this time, he received a wire which mentioned that he had earned a one-hundred-dollar award for *American Blues*. This was followed by a letter from a literary agent, Audrey Wood, who would become his friend and adviser. Around this time, he visited Rose at the sanatorium. He was aghast, finding her not just delusional but also uttering obscenities. In 1939, with the help of Wood, Williams was awarded a one-thousand-dollar grant from the Rockefeller Foundation in recognition of his play *Battle of Angels*. Wood enrolled Williams at a seminar on playwriting under John Gassner and Theresa Hellburn at the New School for Social Research in New York. By this time (i.e. the late 1930s), Williams was "admittedly a homosexual. In 1939, a homosexual was outside the law, outside the Church, branded a pervert by conventional society. This laid a particular onus on Williams, with his religious upbringing, and might account for his deterministic point of view" (Hale 21). In 1940, Williams's play *Battle of Angels* debuted in Boston and flopped. Williams revised it and in 1957 brought it back as *Orpheus Descending*, which was later made into the movie *The Fugitive Kind*, starring Marlon Brando and Anna Magnani. After this failure, Williams again began to drift from one city to another, including Acapulco, before returning to New Orleans. In 1943, Rose had a lobotomy, then thought of as a cure for schizophrenia. The same year, he was asked to report to Hollywood as Audrey Wood secured a contract with MGM for two hundred and fifty dollars a week. She asked for a list of his unpublished works, eager to copyright them. Williams listed more than thirty-five plays, twenty-five stories, and forty pages of verse published in New Directions' *Five Young American Poets*, written since the Mummers days in 1936; there were other items he couldn't recall. And at Audrey Wood's request, he kept on listing the initial drafts for at least five plays which would become landmark plays with innovations which would eventually transform the American stage. The Hollywood venture did not work out. Williams had written a short story titled "Portrait of a Girl in Glass", which he turned into a screenplay titled *The Gentleman Caller*; Williams offered MGM the draft, which was turned down. He, however, claimed that this play would last longer than *Gone with the Wind*. Williams's words eventually turned out to be prophetic. *The Glass Menagerie* was the first play that not just received public attention but also caught the attention of drama critics. It was to become one of the greatest American plays, one of the most anthologised, most performed, and most translated of all American plays.

In order to best understand Tennessee Williams and his most celebrated play *The Glass Menagerie*, it would be wise to analyse and critique the context which led him to write experimental plays. According to David Krasner, American modernism, generally speaking, also commenced at the turn of the century and rose to prominence during the mid-twentieth century. Krasner says that American modernism was defined by:

> liberal values associated with free love, free speech, and, to a certain degree, political anarchy. In addition, there was a rejection of sentimentality that had been characteristic of American provincialism; advocacy of the suffragette movement and women's rights; and commitment to uncovering the "truth" in the human condition. Modernism implied cosmopolitanism, reflecting an emergent urban life and its rising bohemianism (particularly New York City and its downtown artistic scene known as "Greenwich Village"). Modernism brought with it

> a sense of cultural leadership (the feeling that the participants were on the cutting edge of art and literature), and was marked by a determination to be politically and socially relevant to the working class.
>
> (143)

In the first decade of the twentieth century, mainstream American theatre focused primarily on either light comedies or melodramas. Deanna M. Toten Beard says that these plays were "characterized by a kind of pseudo-realism in dialogue and scenic requirements" (54). Certain bold artists who were part of the Little Theatre Movement began to emulate European realism. These plays, says Beard,

> experimented with dreams, nightmares, hallucinations, the psychological, and the illogical. Such plays were also the province of little theatres in America, though, unlike European and European-inspired realist dramas, this kind of experimental drama did not belong to any self-conscious movement of writing.
>
> (54)

Though these plays have usually been ignored or overlooked, one may say that this is how American experimentalism commenced, an experimentalism that eventually led to the evolution of what we now refer to as modern American drama. Interestingly, though American experimentalist playwrights loved stage poetry, they did not write verse drama. Instead, "[t]he poetry of these dramatic experiments was a modern lyricism characterized by rhythm, image, and anxiety" (Beard 54).

Influenced by revolutionary and political ideals, Eugene O'Neill, says Krasner, emerged, as 'the' twentieth-century American dramatist, one who brought a richness of detail and psychological astuteness and profundity for the first time to the American stage. He experimented with the use of masks onstage and, influenced much by Freud introduced inner monologues, established realism in American drama and, most importantly, helped develop a uniquely American brand of expressionism. Originating principally in Germany and Austria, the movement initially was associated with painting and poetry, but the avant-garde style became closely associated with the Weimar culture particularly in and around Berlin; the style soon extended to a wide range of the arts, including music, dance, theatre, and films, and spread to other parts of Europe and America. The expressionist artists sought to depict subjective emotions and responses of individuals instead of objective reality and with the help of grotesque distortions, exaggerations, and fantasy. The depictions therefore would be stark, jarring, and often violent. The purpose was to portray the turmoil or the *angst* of the individual. Krasner says that O'Neill's plays "probe the American Dream, race relations, class conflicts, sexuality, human aspirations, disappointment, alienation, psychoanalysis, and the American family with a thoroughness and intensity at a level his contemporaries could barely contemplate" (143). The Broadway melodramas that O'Neill wrote in the 1920s and 1930s became the finest specimens of American theatre of the period. His melodramas were unconventional; instead of the conventional ones which relied on impending cataclysms, exaggerated emotions, and gaudy and garish exhibitionism, O'Neill's melodramas "conveyed subtler intimacies, personal tragedies, and psychological complexities" (Krasner 143). Through his works, O'Neill primarily sought to pioneer the concept of a modern American drama tradition; he wished to be a contender against modernist European dramatists such as Ibsen, Strindberg, and Shaw, though, for socio-political reasons in the aftermath of World War I, he, like other American playwrights, might have denied having been influenced by German expressionism. In plays like *Emperor Jones*, the influences of German expressionism are obvious, but it should be noted that O'Neill also crafted his own brand of expressionism. One may claim that it was from O'Neill that other American playwrights learnt "powerful psychological engagement, a focus on human relations, a commitment to deeply personal and emotional experiences, an expression of ideas, and an emphasis on authenticity over facade, which are the hallmarks of modernism" (Krasner 144).

Tennessee Williams also forged a unique style. He himself mentioned the influence of three writers on his works—D. H. Lawrence, Hart Crane, and Anton Chekhov—and to this list Gilbert Debussher adds the names "Samuel Beckett, Bertolt Brecht, Jean Cocteau, Federico Garcia Lorca, Eugene O'Neill, Harold Pinter, Luigi Pirandello, Bernard Shaw, August Strindberg, Oscar Wilde, and Thornton Wilder" (56). Williams's experiments with theatrical conventions began from the 1930s. In *Not About Nightingales* (1938), for example, Williams boldly dealt with and personalised issues of the left-wing theatre. He began implementing the techniques of the Federal Theatre Project's Living Newspaper genre which he had learnt at the playwriting course at the University of Iowa. In *Quit Eating*, the prison play, Williams made use of an announcer and captions for each scene, and the audience got to hear the screaming of newspaper headlines and the voices of broadcasters and sirens. And, most importantly, discarding the traditional five-act structure, he presented his plays as a series of episodes, set in the warden's office and in the cells. Influenced heavily by O'Neill, Williams began to forge a new style combining realism with expressionism. His technique also came quite close to Clifford Odets's realistic technique with which he meant to induce empathy in the audience in *Waiting for Lefty* (1935). Indeed, Williams learnt much from the practitioners of political theatre, Erwin Piscator and Bertolt Brecht, including the use of the screen device, says Payal Nagpal, but she mentions, "these writers used such devices in the context of committee theatre" (xxii), whereas Williams borrowed these ideas and, coupled with the use of expressionistic devices, "created a diffused realism" (xxii). In fact, he worked with Piscator for a while in the early 1940s at the New School for Social Research, but Williams came to detest the idea of inducing political messages into the minds of the audience. He liked the use of film sequences and titles in Picador's plays, however. In Williams's plays, the magic-lantern slide projections, instead of bearing political messages, bore the magic of the unconscious mind and of dreams.

In the use of the magic-lantern slide projections, David Savran finds the influence of surrealism. Savran says,

> Williams's use of 'magic-lantern slides' in *Menagerie* has little in common with the projections and distortions of individual experience and subjectivity that constitute expressionist drama. Rather, it seems far more closely allied to the techniques of surrealism as developed in France in the 1920s and 1930s.
>
> (94)

As he rightly points out, surrealism, unlike expressionism, reached America late. In the early 1930s, there were quite a number of minor exhibitions of work by surrealists in New York, and in 1936, there was a show of Fantastic Art, Dada, and Surrealism at the Museum of Modern Art in New York. In 1941, the Museum of Modern Art held an exhibition of paintings by Joan Miro and Salvador Dali. From the early 1940s, surrealism began to exert a major influence on American artists as a consequence of the immense wartime mobility of European artists and intellectuals.

Speaking about the historical context in which *The Glass Menagerie* is set, Delma E. Presley states that the Great Depression was unexpected. She writes:

> Americans had been told the thirties would be a decade of peace and prosperity. In his final message to Congress on 4 December 1928, President Calvin Coolidge said that citizens should 'regard the present with satisfaction and anticipate the future with optimism.' Coolidge was succeeded by Herbert Hoover who predicted that poverty would soon be virtually non-existent. Even after the Wall Street crash of 24 and 29 October 1929, government officials continued to speak optimistically about the future. According to Andrew Mellon, secretary of the treasury, the economic situation was not 'menacing'; certainly nothing 'warrants pessimism,' he concluded.
>
> (1–2)

In spite of the false optimism, the nationwide trend was definitely not encouraging. Presley adds, "Between 1929 and 1932, the national income fell from $81 billion to $41 billion. Wages declined by 60 percent" (2).

Williams's *Menagerie*, based on ground realities that cultured and educated families were forced to witness in the troubled 1940s, deals with the profound loss that each character in this American middle-class family experiences. Tom Wingfield refers to the socio-political background in his opening speech. He says:

> To begin with, I turn back time. I reverse it to that quaint period, the thirties, when the huge middle class of America was matriculating in a school for the blind. Their eyes had failed them or they had failed their eyes, and so they were having their fingers pressed forcibly down on the fiery Braille alphabet of a dissolving economy.
>
> In Spain there was revolution. Here there was only shouting and confusion. In Spain there was Guernica. Here there were disturbances of labor, sometimes pretty violent, in otherwise peaceful cities such as Chicago, Cleveland, Saint Louis …
>
> This is the social background of the play.
>
> (5)

The post-war era, the 1940s and '50s, became even more unsettling. Thomas Adler states that, if the play were set twenty years later, and if Tom were called upon to provide a capsule overview of the 1940s and 1950s, he might have commented:

> Abroad there was Pearl Harbor, the Holocaust, the Bomb, the Iron Curtain, Korea, Hungary and Suez, the Cold War, and Sputnik. At home there was internment of Japanese-Americans, investigations of suspected Communists, suburban sprawl, rock'n'roll, the ascendency of TV, and racial unrest. America was poised and waiting for upheaval.
>
> (1)

Low economic resources have always been a bane for ambitious young family members in any culture, as their targets and dreams become intangible. In *Menagerie*, a family experiences tensions and frustrations emanating from a lack of economic resources. This leads to the members being dissatisfied, aggressive, and depressed. All three members in this family-centric play are fractured individuals entrapped in their personal agonies and sense of failure.

In an interview with R. C. Lewis in 1947, Williams said that, in *The Glass Menagerie*, he intended to hold the audience "through the revelation of quiet and ordinary truths" (Quoted in Single 192). To reveal such quiet and ordinary truths, Williams conceptualised a new 'plastic theatre,' a term which he used in the Production Notes to *The Glass Menagerie*. It was with *Menagerie* that he began experimenting with and formulating a new dramatic structure.

Collaborating with lighting designer Jo Mielziner and director Elia Kazan, Williams kept on modifying his theatrical idiom for about a decade and a half. Though his plays were vehicles of realism, his vision as a playwright was subjective. And, formulating a new aesthetic, as Robert Bray mentions in his Introduction,

> [a]n habitué of the movies since his childhood, Williams was now experimenting with a more fluid dramatic structure that would to some extent emulate the cinematic technique of *mise-en-scène*, the method by which a film director stages an event for the camera.
>
> (ix)

He made the use of gauze and legends in *Menagerie* and in *A Streetcar Named Desire* (1947). In *A Streetcar Named Desire*, Mielziner designed a fully transparent stage that made it possible for the audience to visualise the stages of mental derangement of Blanche DuBois. This again shows the juxtaposition of expressionistic conventions with realistic ones. In the 1950s, complex sexual issues and homosexuality featured in his plays, including famous plays like *Cat on a Hot Tin Roof* (1955), a time when Williams himself was preoccupied with his own sexual identity.

Williams wrote, re-wrote, and produced a play doubly titled *The Two-Character Play* and *Outcry*, though unsuccessfully, from 1967 to 1975. *The Two-Character Play* in many ways is similar to *Menagerie*. Brenda Murphy calls it a "highly symbolic monodrama about the artist" and adds that "the play makes use of the brother-sister dyad that pervaded Williams's imagination" (189). Actors and siblings Felice and Clare find themselves abandoned by the other members of their theatrical troupe in a theatre on the road. Though Clare initially shows reluctance, eventually she agrees to Felice's suggestion that they put on Felice's play about the two of them. In the play-within-the-play, they fail to leave the house where their parents shot each other. It remains unclear whether their father shot his spouse and then himself or their mother did. The play-within-the-play, it turns out, has no ending, and the siblings find themselves trapped in the theatre. Like his parents, Felice raises a revolver to shoot Clare but fails. The siblings raise their hands instead and embrace each other. *The Two-Character Play*, like *The Glass Menagerie*, is endless and has a similar ending. In both, the male protagonist, like the playwright himself, fails to purge himself of guilt feelings after having dissociated himself from his family.

As Peter Davison mentions, "[n]o Western nation has shown itself so sharply divided in its attitude to live theatre drama as has the United States" (553). Calling the United States the land par excellence of Show Biz, Davison adds, "from minstrel shows to musicals, from Broadway to Hollywood, from Chautauqua to vaudeville, it has ridden high in vitality, excitement, and sheer panache, supremely self-confident" (553). Davison calls Tennessee Williams, of all modern dramatists, the most "colourful, varied and prolific in output," one who "took risks in his drama" (554), a risk-taking that began with *The Glass Menagerie*, which premiered in the Civic Theatre in Chicago on 26 December 1944. This show was directed by Eddie Dowling and Margo Jones. The cast for the opening night had Eddie Dowling as Tom Wingfield, Laurette Taylor as Amanda Wingfield, Julie Haydon as Laura Wingfield, and Anthony Ross as Jim O'Connor. After a shaky start, the play was championed by Chicago critics Ashton Stevens and Claudia Cassidy. In effect, though the audience initially was sparse, soon it became a hit of the season. *The Glass Menagerie* opened on Broadway in the Playhouse Theatre on 31 March 1945 and played there until 29 June 1946. It then moved to the Royale Theatre from 1 July 1946 until its closing on 3 August 1946. The play won the New York Drama Critics' Circle Award in 1945. Two years later, *A Streetcar Named Desire* opened, surpassing his previous success and securing his status as one of the country's best playwrights, earning Williams a Drama Critics' Award and his first Pulitzer Prize. Williams won the same set of prizes again in 1955 for *Cat on a Hot Tin Roof*. Other hits from the 1950s included *Camino Real* (1953) and *Sweet Bird of Youth* (1959). In *Camino Real* and some later plays, Williams kept on implementing non-realistic styles as expressionism and surrealism, and the plays from 1945 to 1961 gained immense popularity.

The 1960s were difficult times for Williams. His success began to wane, and the plays began to receive dismal reviews. He suffered from intense depression after the death of his partner in 1961, and in 1969 he had to be hospitalised. The playwright continued to dabble in alcohol and drugs, though he kept on writing. A nearly empty bottle of wine and unidentified capsules were found beneath Williams's body as he died in his suite at the Hotel Elysée in New York on February 25 1983.

Bibliography

References

Adler, Thomas P. *American Drama, 1940–1960: A Critical History*. Twayne, 1994.

Davison, Peter. "Tennessee Williams, Arthur Miller, and Edward Albee." *The Pelican Guide to English Literature*, Vol. 9, American Literature, edited by Boris Ford, Penguin, 1991, pp. 553–63.

Debussher, Gilbert. "On American and European Influences." *Tennessee Williams's The Glass Menagerie*, Edited & with an Introduction by Harold Bloom, Infobase Publishing-Chelsea House, 2007, pp. 56–63.

Hale, Allean. "Early Williams: The Making of a Playwright." *The Cambridge Companion to Tennessee Williams*, edited by Matthew C. Roudane, Cambridge University Press, 1997, pp. 11–28.

Krasner, David, editor. *A Companion to Twentieth-Century American Drama*. Blackwell Publishing, 2005; Beard, Deanna M. Toten. "American Experimentalism, American Expressionism, and Early O'Neill." Krasner, pp. 53–68; Krasner, David. "Eugene O'Neill: American Drama and American Modernism." Krasner, pp. 142–158; Murphy, Brenda. "Tennessee Williams." Krasner, pp. 175–191.

Nagpal, Payal, editor. *Tennessee Williams's The Glass Menagerie*. Worldview, 2016; Nagpal, Payel. "Introduction." Nagpal, pp. xi–xlvii; Single, Lori Leathers. "Flying the Jolly Roger: Images of Escape and Selfhood in Tennessee Williams's The Glass Menagerie." Nagpal, pp. 185–205.

Presley, Delma E. *The Glass Menagerie: An American Memory*. Twayne Publishers - G. K. Hall & Co, 1990.

Reid, Desmond. "Tennessee Williams." *Studies: An Irish Quarterly Review*, Vol. 46, No. 184, 1957, pp. 431–46. *JSTOR*, http://www.jstor.org/stable/30098928. Accessed 3 Mar. 2024.

Savran, David. *Communists, Cowboys, and Queers: The Politics of Masculinity in the Work of Arthur Miller and Tennessee Williams*. University of Minnesota Press, 1992.

Williams, Tennessee. *The Glass Menagerie*, edited and with an introduction by Robert Bray, New Directions, 1999.

2 Autobiographical Elements in *The Glass Menagerie*

When we think of autobiographical elements in *The Glass Menagerie*, the first thing that strikes us is the name of the narrator protagonist. Williams was named Thomas Lanier Williams by his parents at birth, and his nickname had been Tom. Stephen J. Bottoms rightly says that this awareness instantly alerts us to the possibility that Tom Wingfield is a depiction of Tennessee Williams and that *The Glass Menagerie* is Tennessee Williams's "most blatantly autobiographical play" (*Handbook* 41). Williams remarked once that if it were true that all of his works were autobiographical, it was equally true that none of his works was. Bottoms adds, however, that though the play drew much from personal experiences, "[t]he events of the play are not revelations of a personal history but the component parts of a distinct, poetic vision dealing with themes of memory and loss, isolation and interdependence" (*Handbook* 41) amongst other things.

Cornelius Williams moved his family to St. Louis, Missouri in 1918 to a tenement at 6544 Enright Avenue, having taken a managerial position in a shoe company, very similar to the one described in *Menagerie*. The first thing that Williams drew from life and transformed was the Wingfield apartment, "one of those vast hive-like conglomerations of cellular living-units that flower as warty growths in overcrowded urban centers of lower middle class population" (3). Though Cornelius had a fairly good salary, this move made Tennessee Williams aware for the first time of the squalor of lower-middle-class life. Their middle-class apartment became the cramped and ugly tenement in the play. Caught in the marital tension between his parents, the boy Williams used to run away to the Forest Park Zoo. This very well could have served as the analogy of the menagerie. From their home, they could hear strains of music from a nearly ballroom; this became the music from Paradise Dance Hall in the play.

Mr. Wingfield senior, in *Menagerie*, is shown to have abandoned his family years back. In real life, however, Cornelius Williams had left his job with the telephone company and had taken another with the International Shoe Company in St. Louis. To Cornelius Williams, "St. Louis was the city

DOI: 10.4324/9781003504245-3

of opportunity, in 1918 fifth largest in the United States, with a fine school system, universities, libraries, a famed symphony orchestra, a splendid art museum" (Hale 13). Indeed, Cornelius had never abandoned his wife and children, the effect of which was probably worse on their children because of his constant bickering with his wife. Their life together had unfortunately become a battleground, and caught in the midst of parents with completely opposite natures, Williams felt trapped. Another thing that enhanced the slipping away of Williams's emotional equilibrium was the coercion on his father's part to make him join the shoe company during his first stint of university education. Williams later classified this time as the most miserable two years of his life. The wage-earning experience took a toll on his mental health just as it does to Tom. He put much of himself in Tom Wingfield, loathing his clerical job and squirming to escape.

Among the many things that Williams drew from personal experiences, the most distressing was his interactions with his mother, Edwina Dakin Williams. Edwina incessantly kept on reminiscing about her life and the experiences in her youth in the Deep South. The daughter of an episcopal minister, the Reverend Walter Dakin, she almost had an idyllic life. As Hale mentions, "[h]is mother Edwina, had the beauty and social inclinations of a Southern belle and, if not the wealth, the status that the Episcopalian ministry held in the small cotton center of Clarksdale, Mississippi" (11). She often performed as a singer and, after graduating from high school, worked hard to keep alive the traditions of the antebellum (i.e. pre-Civil War) South, belonging to the last generation that continued to make that tremendous attempt. If Amanda Wingfield boasts of seventeen gentlemen callers, it would actually be quite unimpressive in comparison with Edwina Dakin; the Dakin family accounts show that Edwina on one occasion received thirty gentlemen callers in a single day. Edwina Dakin, just like Amanda Wingfield, committed the mistake of falling in love with the wrong man and the mistake of choosing the wrong man as her husband amongst her many gentlemen callers. She fell in love with and chose as her life partner Cornelius Coffin Williams, a travelling salesman with the Cumberland Telephone and Telegraph Company, a man "in love with long distances" (5), just like Amanda Wingfield's husband. After marriage, the long-distance man continued to travel while Edwina lived in Clarksdale, Mississippi, fictionalised as Blue Mountain in *Menagerie*. Eventually, Cornelius Williams moved his entire family to St. Louis, Missouri, a state that was neither northern nor southern, one which had been a free state during the Civil War. Thrust in such an environment, Edwina felt totally alienated. Hale mentions that she "felt herself a nobody and, with a sort of reverse snobbery, impressed on her children that in St. Louis only money and status mattered" (13). The only thing she was left with were memories of her beautiful past, and she constantly idealised and reminisced over her past just as Amanda Wingfield does in the play.

The prototype for Laura was Williams's sister, Rose. The child Tennessee was quiet and observant in contrast to Rose, who was lively and spirited. Williams's attachment to his sister was tremendous; as Hale mentions, the siblings "only sixteen months apart, were as inseparable as twins, and were called 'The Couple'. They were so attuned that when one was ill, the other developed symptoms" (11). Rose, like Laura, loved playing old records on the Victrola record player and often taught her brother the dance steps she knew. Like Laura, she too had enrolled in the Rubicam's Business College to learn typing and shorthand but had quit abruptly, unable to cope with the pressure. And just like Laura in the play, she kept this a secret from their mother Edwina, wandered about in the city, and returned home late in the afternoons with the pretence of having attended her classes. Another important event drawn from life was the event of arranging a gentleman caller for Rose. Tom's wage of sixty-five dollars a month matches Williams's own wage in the International Shoe Company, and one of his co-workers was a man named Jim Connor. Williams and Connor were part of the same college fraternity. At their mother Edwina's insistence, Williams invited Jim Connor to dinner only to discover that he was already engaged, just like Jim O'Connor in *Menagerie*. Interestingly, another of his co-workers was a man named Stanley Kowalski, a name he immortalised in another play, *A Streetcar Named Desire*, considered to be one of his best. Another thing definitely needs mention. Unlike Laura, Rose was far from being shy and demure; in fact, in real life, she was much like their extrovert and talkative mother Amanda. Sprightly and vivacious, she had no trouble at all attracting men in her teens and early twenties, and she enjoyed the attention of young men whom she dated, and she even listed records of them in her journal, though none of those men manifested a steady interest in her. Yet, as Bottoms states, "by twenty-four she was in danger of being 'left on the shelf'; hence her mother's campaign" (*Handbook* 43). At the age of twenty-four, she sexually propositioned a colleague of Thomas's from the shoe company, one of the men she dated. Their brother Dakin has mentioned that Thomas was much shocked and that he told her clearly that he was disgusted with her behaviour. Laura's physical deformity, as opposed to Rose's lack of mental equilibrium, made the re-telling of the family story less harsh.

Rose and Thomas Williams did attend the Soldan High School in St. Louis but only for a year, and then the siblings began to go to different schools. Williams makes Laura and Tom attend the same school until their pre-graduation years in the play, and that added more poignance to Jim the gentleman caller's visit. In the Laura–Jim conversations, the nickname Blue Roses gains an amount of significance coupled with an element of pathos. In real life, Williams had heard this anecdote from a childhood friend whose father was a surgeon. This gentleman had

German-speaking patients who often misunderstood his English; and in one instance, they misheard 'pleurosis' as 'blue roses.' As Bottoms states, it was Williams's way of taking, "what had been a private joke and give it a poetic resonance" (*Handbook* 43).

Williams mentioned that his family lived in a tenement not unlike the one shown in *The Glass Menagerie*. He also mentioned that his sister's room was painted white and had shelves which he had helped her fill with little glass animals which made up Rose's menagerie. Williams adds,

> She was the member of the family with whom I was most in sympathy and, looking back, her glass menagerie had a meaning for me ... and as I thought about it the glass animals came to represent the fragile, delicate ties that must be broken, that you inevitably break, when you try to fulfil yourself.
>
> (quoted in Bigsby 37)

Williams's biographer Lyle Leverich, however, refuses to accept this story, saying that the dramatist often dramatised himself by fabricating stories. In fact, Thomas's younger brother Dakin mentioned that Rose did have glass trinkets, "just two or three pieces ... very cheap little things, probably purchased at Woolworth's" (quoted in Bottoms, *Handbook* 44). A menagerie actually belonged to a lady named Mrs. Maggie Wingfield in Clarksdale, and she kept her menagerie of glass animals on display in her front window.

And, finally, as Nancy M. Tischler rightly says, Williams was quintessentially American "but never a typical pragmatic middle American. He saw himself as an archetypal outsider" (147). Tom Wingfield, in the play, exudes this vibe of being an outsider, his detachment obvious right from the moment we meet him. Tennessee Williams was a typical Southerner, as Tischler says: "[a] Southerner who lamented the loss of a dignity, elegance, and sense of honour, he was never satisfied with the dreary present and its flat speech" (147–148). He manifested a love for everything that may be referred to as quintessentially romantic. Tischler continues:

> Williams yearned for "long distance," for "cloudy symbols of high romance," or what romantics call the "yonder bank." His characters love a lost, idealised past ("Blue Mountain"), and they live for a dangerous, problematic future ("Terra Incognita"). From beginning to end, Williams's theatrical struggle was also a romantic quest for Parnassus. It was romantic dreamers — quixotic and tattered old warriors, fragile young poets, frightened misfits — whom he celebrated in his poems, stories, novels and plays. Romanticism was the very fabric of his life and work — woven throughout.
>
> (148)

Williams presented himself as a 'romantic loner' to his agent Audrey Wood. This kind of romanticism is captured in *Menagerie* too. Along with this romanticism comes the urge to place his family history within the context of significant events in world history. Setting the play in 1937 and 1938, he makes the references to the Spanish Civil War, the bombing of Guernica, and British Prime Minister Neville Chamberlain's endeavours to pacify Adolf Hitler. As Bottoms says, "Williams wanted to parallel the domestic crisis of the play with far greater crises in the world at large, creating an interwoven narrative of public and private calamity" (*Handbook* 45). In fact, from around this time, Williams began battling acute crises at home. When Williams went away to the University of Iowa in the fall of 1937, Rose had to be sent away to the Farmington State Hospital for schizophrenia. From this point on, Williams would be plagued and tormented by the fear of insanity as mental illness afflicted both sides of the family. In the words of Harry Rasky, Rose's confinement was indeed a hard blow as "Tom and Rose were like Siamese twins joined at the heart" (quoted in Hale 17). When he visited her in the sanatorium, she was already delusional and schizophrenic, and he was shocked to find her uttering obscenities, which he was unaware that she knew. And by the time he wrote the play, in 1943, Rose had been lobotomised. Tom's family did not tell him of the operation until after it was done, yet he always felt guilty about having been unable to prevent it. He had not seen her for quite a few years, but she was forever in his mind. It is no wonder that Tom says in the play, "Oh, Laura, Laura, I tried to leave you behind me, but I am more faithful than I intended to be!" (97).

Bibliography

Primary Text

Williams, Tennessee. *The Glass Menagerie*, edited by Stephen J. Bottoms, Methuen Drama India-Bloomsbury, 2015.

References

Bottoms, Stephen J. "The Glass Menagerie." *A Student Handbook to the Plays of Tennessee Williams*, edited by Katherine Weiss, Methuen Drama India-Bloomsbury, 2021, pp. 17–82.

Roudane, Matthew C., editor. *The Cambridge Companion to Tennessee Williams*. Cambridge University Press, 1997; Bigsby, C.W.E. "Entering The Glass Menagerie". Roudane, pp. 29–44; Hale, Allean. "Early Williams: the making of a playwright". Roudane, pp. 11–28; Tischler, Nancy M. "Romantic textures in Tennessee Williams's plays and short stories". Roudane, pp. 147–166.

3 Tennessee Williams, the Southern Writer

Tennessee Williams has often been compared to other writers of the South, sometimes also to the novelist William Faulkner. Both the Mississippi-born writers found grand subject matter in the history and the contemporaneity of the South. Williams was deeply indebted to Southern literary conventions. Kimball King opines that the playwright's criticisms of the South, both overt and covert, are often harsh, "but his continuing love/hate relationship with the culture he was born into provides dramatic conflict and excitement to everything he wrote" (627). Williams's plays reflect many of the characteristics of Southern writers which anticipate the postmodern dilemma. The era in *The Glass Menagerie*, the thirties, witnessed the integration and growth of the formerly despised middle class. As Tom Wingfield says at the outset, the time is turned back to "when the huge middle class of America was matriculating in a school for the blind" (5). Most of Williams's plays reflected binaries which were praised or satirised in Southern writing; King mentions "agrarianism vs. urbanism, the New South vs. the Antebellum, and the chevalier vs. the upstart" (627). Williams was a man who took pride in his own 'aristocratic' connections in the feudalistic South; one of his ancestors was chancellor of the Southwest Territory, and two others were a senator and a governor of Tennessee. Yet, as a realist, he decided not to depict the Southern elite idealistically, as Margaret Mitchell had done. Mitchell's novel *Gone with the Wind* became a bestseller, and the motion picture based on the novel gained worldwide recognition. The novel and the picture propagated and perpetuated certain stereotypical myths and assumptions about Southern culture, however. King says,

> Williams had to choose between perpetuating Mitchell's stereotypes or shattering them. In Mitchell's pages, plantation life is perceived to have been lavish, almost regal. Slaves are seldom mistreated and, consequently, loyal to their owners; Northerners are mainly predators who ruthlessly destroy a genteel civilization.
>
> (630)

DOI: 10.4324/9781003504245-4

Williams manages to portray the charm of Southern culture, yet he deconstructs it in play after play. The tension between a Southerner's dream of an idyllic life and the reality of the life he actually lives breathes energy into all of Williams's art. Williams's male protagonists do not fit into the constructs of the stereotypical Southern hero, however. Instead of abandoning the concept of the hero, he adapted it to fit the hapless hero into a world which was hopelessly corrupt, violent, and unjust.

Louis D. Rubin, Jr. was one of the first critics to evaluate these Southern writers writing after the First World War. This is how he defined their common attributes:

> All tended to ground their writings in their regional experience. However much they differed as individual, original artists, their works seemed to share many characteristics, including some that were largely lacking in other American writers of the period: a sense of the past, an uninhibited reliance upon the full resources of language and (the old-fashioned moral absolutes that lay behind such language), an attitude toward evil as being present not only in economic or social forces but integral to the "fallen state" of humankind, an ability to get at the full complexity of a situation rather than seeming to reduce it to its simplified essentials, a suspicion of abstractions, a bias in favor of the individual, the concrete, the unique, even the exaggerated and outlandish in human portraiture.
>
> (quoted in King 628)

This analysis is so apt when applied to Williams. In most of his plays, the personal dilemmas and social predicaments are inextricably linked with the South. *A Streetcar Named Desire* posits a contrast between members of the fallen aristocracy and those of the new industrial order; *Cat on a Hot Tin Roof* portrays the nouveau riche; *Last Summer* also contrasts licentious Southern aristocrats with power and pelf against their poor relations. Like other Southern writers, Faulkner and Walker Percy, Williams manifests a belief in the metaphorical importance of the South, viewing it as a doomed civilisation yet carrying the elegance and legacy of the past. He condemns the culture's exclusionary elements and its denial of plurality, two of the causes that led to its demise. In Williams's plays, grounded in the regional experience, the past always influences the lives of the protagonists. None of Williams's characters can escape the burdens of their personal and regional histories. Thomas Adler speaks about the issue thus: "The tension between these two cultures, an agrarian South that looked back nostalgically to a partly mythical past of gentility and refinement and an industrialized North that rewarded business acumen and practicality, would haunt Williams throughout his life" (131). Adler notes that Williams always denied any "acquaintance with political and social dialectics" (132) and claimed "Humanitarian" (132) as his only party affiliation, yet he believed that no "writer has much purpose back of him unless he feels bitterly the inequities of the society he lives in" (quoted in Adler 132). Away from crass materialism, said Williams,

> the South once had a way of life that I am just old enough to remember—a culture that had grace, elegance .. an inbred culture ... not a society based on money, as in the North. I write out of regret for that [and] of the forces that have destroyed it.... I write about the South because I think the war between romanticism and the hostility to it is very sharp there.
>
> (quoted in Adler 132–133)

When Williams began to be branded as the 'Southern' playwright, he started transferring situations and characters from St. Louis, a locale he dreaded as the city of St. Pollution, to a Southern setting. Many of Williams's plays also draw on New Orleans, which makes him adhere to the 'deep' South. C. Hugh Holman points out that the South was composed of three regions: the Tidewater, the Piedmont and the 'deep' South. Small-town Southern life, with its class segregation, resembles the Piedmont tradition. *The Glass Menagerie* would fall under the Piedmont category. Amanda Wingfield is a fine example of the conservative patriarchal feudalistic South with its hypocritical denial of sexuality. In his plays, Williams questions the patriarchal set-up of the Old South, the sense of hierarchy in the Old South and the subjugation of black people, both the deification and subjugation of women, the corrupting power of wealth, the obsession with keeping up appearances in sync with the old paternalistic order, and the sense of guilt related to the acknowledgement of sexuality. Williams also brings to our attention many corruptions and vices related to the rigid gender stereotypes prevalent in the South. Williams exposes the hypocrisy of a society, with a patriarchal set-up, which denies a woman's sexuality; it is a society in which men dominate women to prove their manhood. Men, in fact, indulge in being vulgar and crude by boasting openly about their sexuality: Val, for example, in *The Battle of Angels*, Stanley in *Streetcar*, and Big Daddy in *Cat on a Hot Tin Roof.* In sharp contrast, we find Lucretia Collins in *Portrait of a Madonna* and the immensely famous Blanche DuBois in *A Streetcar Named Desire*, who have to deny their strong sexual needs and maintain a clean and chaste image in public. Amanda Wingfield shows displeasure at Tom reading *Lady Chatterley's Lover*, "that hideous book by that insane Mr. Lawrence" (21). The lives of individuals are weighed down by the class and racial segregations, behavioural traits, and taboos which form an inevitable part of Southern history and culture. These affect personal resolutions and moral choices. Italians are mistreated, for example, in *The Battle of Angels* and *The Rose Tattoo*. In this world, defiance of the social code shows the risk of personal annihilation. Moreover, says King, hierarchy seems to have a connection with the Anglo-Saxons, a view shared by Henry Popkin. In the 'deep' South, many aristocratic Creole families were often of French or Spanish ancestry and thus this society was not shaped entirely by Anglo-Saxon ethics or codes of conduct. Popkin says, "the Southern aristocrats are challenged, sometimes by upstarts of Anglo-Saxon descent but more often by newcomers who bear Italian, Polish, or Jewish names" (56). Such challengers are present in almost every one of Williams's plays. Popkin reminds us, however, that though the challengers are ubiquitous, they are often not deliberately hostile. In *The Glass Menagerie*, for example, the Wingfields constantly have to encounter this non-Anglo-Saxon bunch. Tom Wingfield's boss in the warehouse is named Mendoza; Amanda purchases food items from Garfinkel's Delicatessen, to which she owes a hefty sum of money, and ironically she awaits her dinner guest, Jim O'Connor, the Irish Catholic gentleman caller, for her daughter Laura. Though Jim works in the same factory as Amanda's son, he tries to build himself up subscribing to the American dream, the dream of success. His preparations to rise in the competitive corporate world are contrasted with the laid-back attitude of the Wingfields. Popkin says, "[t]he use of foreign names and foreign characters is part of Williams's complex symbolic system. The foreign name means *life*; the Anglo-Saxon name may mean *stagnation*" (57).

Frank Durham and other critics opine that the exquisite poetic qualities in Williams's language come from his Southern origin. Durham writes:

> He takes colloquial speech, often the colloquial speech of the South, and through a keen ear for its rhythms and patterns, its imagery and symbolism, lifts it to the level of poetry. It is real speech, but real speech intensified and heightened so that it not only evokes the pleasure of recognition but communicates the inexpressible, the very essence of character, emotion, and situation in a way traditionally associated with poetry.
>
> (67–68)

The Glass Menagerie, along with his other plays, is full of exquisitely poetic passages. Referring to Williams's long line, Marion Migid says that it "achieves its most striking effects through a Steinian repetitiveness, through the use of unexpected archaisms, and the insertion of unexpected 'literary' words and ironically elegant turns of phrase" (quoted in Durham, 69–70). Awaiting the gentleman caller for her daughter, Amanda re-lives her past, also taking out an old dress that she wore to impress the young Mr. Wingfield, Rose and Tom's father. The conversation runs:

> This is the dress in which I led the cotillion. Won the cakewalk twice at Sunset Hill, wore one Spring to the Governor's Ball in Jackson! See how I sashayed around the ballroom, Laura? … I wore it on Sundays for my gentlemen callers! I had it on the day I met your father. … I had malaria fever all that spring. The change of climate from East Tennessee to the Delta—weakened resistance. I had a little temperature all the time—not enough to be serious—just enough to make me restless and giddy! Invitations poured in—parties all over the Delta! "Stay in bed," said Mother, "you have a fever!"—but I just wouldn't. I took quinine but kept on going, going! Evenings, dances! Afternoons, long, long rides! Picnics—lovely! So lovely, that country in May—all lacy with dogwood, literally flooded with jonquils! That was the spring I had the craze for jonquils. Jonquils became an absolute obsession. Mother said, "Honey, there's no more room for jonquils." And still I kept on bringing in more jonquils. Whenever, wherever I saw them, I'd say, "Stop! Stop! I see jonquils!" I made the young men help me gather the jonquils! It was a joke, Amanda and her jonquils. Finally there were no more vases to hold them, every available space was filled with jonquils. No vases to hold them? All right, I'll hold them myself! And then I—… met your father! Malaria fever and jonquils and then—this—boy. …
> (53–54)

Durham rightly says that her words have "the patterned construction of a poem" (68), the rhythms portraying the emotions of the speaker. Moreover, the passage is a beautiful description of the lost glory of the Southern past. Williams invokes exquisitely beautiful floral imagery to enhance the poetic resonance of the passage.

Tom's language, like his mother's, is remarkably Southern too. This is how he announces the arrangement he has made for the Gentleman Caller.

> *TOM:* We are going to have one.
> *AMANDA:* *What*?
> *TOM:* A gentleman caller!
> …
> *AMANDA:* You mean you have asked some nice young man to come over?
> *TOM:* Yep. I've asked him to dinner.
> *AMANDA:* You really did?
> *TOM:* I did.
> *AMANDA:* You did, and did he—*accept*?

TOM:	He did!
AMANDA:	Well, well—well, well! That's lovely!
TOM:	I thought that you would be pleased.
AMANDA:	It's definite then?
TOM:	Very definite.
AMANDA:	Soon?
TOM:	Very soon.

(41)

This exchange of dialogue shows a repetitive rhythmic flow of words, almost like refrains. Durham says, "[h]ere is approximately the give-and-take of traditional stichomythia" (69).

The ending of the play is poignant too. Tom says in his closing speech:

> I left Saint Louis. I descended the step of this fire escape for a last time and followed, from then on, in my father's footsteps, attempting to find in motion what was lost in space. I travelled around a great deal. The cities swept about me like dead leaves, leaves that were brightly coloured but torn away from the branches. I would have stopped, but I was pursued by something. It always came upon me unawares, taking me altogether by surprise. Perhaps it was a familiar bit of music. Perhaps it was only a piece of transparent glass. Perhaps I am walking along a street at night, in some strange city, before I have found companions. I pass the lighted window of a shop where perfume is sold. The window is filled with pieces of coloured glass, tiny transparent bottles in delicate colors, like bits of a shattered rainbow.
>
> (96–97)

The closing speech catches the same colloquial tone as found in the stichomythic exchanges of words and shows the Southern rhythmic pattern, yet the speech gathers acute sensitivity because it is heavy with the emotions of the speaker.

Bibliography

Primary Text

Williams, Tennessee. *The Glass Menagerie*, edited by Stephen J. Bottoms, Methuen Drama India-Bloomsbury, 2015.

References

Adler, Thomas P. *American Drama, 1940–1960: A Critical History*. Twayne, 1994.

Durham, Frank. "Tennessee Williams, Theatre Poet in Prose." *Modern Critical Interpretations: Tennessee Williams's The Glass Menagerie*, edited and with an introduction by Harold Bloom, Chelsea House Publishers, 1988, pp. 59–73.

King, Kimball. "Tennessee Williams: A Southern Writer." *The Mississippi Quarterly*, Vol. 48, No. 4, 1995, pp. 627–47. *JSTOR*, http://www.jstor.org/stable/26475760. Accessed 4 Mar. 2024.

Popkin, Henry. "The Plays of Tennessee Williams." *The Tulane Drama Review*, Vol. 4, No. 3, 1960, pp. 45–64. *JSTOR*, https://doi.org/10.2307/1124844. Accessed 4 Mar. 2024.

4 Williams's Play with Time

The Glass Menagerie as a Memory Play

In *The Glass Menagerie*, Tennessee Williams has a wonderful play with the sense of time. Tom Wingfield begins the play by declaring, "I turn back time" (5), making it clear that the audience is going to witness his memory of his family. This declaration takes the audience back to the past: "the thirties, when the huge middle class of America was matriculating in a school for the blind" (5). Sam Bluefarb brings our attention to Tom's expository confessions and Amanda's spiralling monologues, stating that through them, "Williams probes through a two-fold layer of time" (514). As Tom declares, the play's actions are set in the 1930s, but once the spectators are taken to that era, they are taken back further, through Amanda, to a time even more remote. Yet this play is not a typical play associated with the protagonist reminiscing over the past. The play also expresses the present that Tom now inhabits. Edgardo Dela Cruz opines that the play "operates on two levels—the farther and the nearer past" (248), the remote past motivating the characters and the closer one constituting the play's action. In addition, Williams's manifestation of the past in *The Glass Menagerie* is varied, involving individual memories. For Amanda, it is her precious Southern era with her seventeen gentlemen callers; and for Laura, it is her high school crush for Jim. As Tom keeps on presenting "truth in the pleasant disguise of illusion" (4), the personal past and the accompanying *angst* (his own and theirs) become universal.

> Time past and time future
> What might have been and what has been
> Point to one end, which is always present…

Quoting these words of T.S. Eliot from "Four Quartets", Sam Bluefarb says that "[t]he effort to escape both the restrictions of time and its demands forms the thematic and motivational basis" (513) of the play. Eventually, all three—Amanda, Tom, and Laura Wingfield—fail in their attempts to escape and break their bonds. Each one remains time-bound in a different way. The Wingfields surprisingly do not live in the present

DOI: 10.4324/9781003504245-5

at all, and the past and the future that occupy their minds somehow do not accommodate a present for them to inhabit. Bluefarb adds,

> [t]he past not only casts its shadow upon the present and the future, but actually determines the course that each of these shall take. Thus the present and, by implication, the future are prevented from taking a course. For while the future has yet to be born, the present is a static, stillborn entity.
>
> (513)

The mother, Amanda, keeps on yearning for the past. Because of the flow of time, her attempts of living in the past are virtually impossible, yet she remains emotionally tied to the past. Amanda's past is unmistakably tied to a sense of nostalgia, a past through which she wishes to embellish the present as well as the future. Though she lives in the present, she evaluates her present in terms of the past. Middle-aged and a mother of two, she remains trapped in the time when she was a vivacious Southern belle. Her Tennessee girlhood and adolescence with the rich and impressive gentlemen callers remain alive in her memories. Unfortunately, Amanda fails to let go of her past and come to terms with life in the present, and this is what eventually spoils her own and her children's future—the future which is the present time in the play when Tom is speaking about his mother and his sister as they appear in his memories. It is for her that the future, no matter how much she shows concern, becomes implausible and bleak. Tom eagerly looks towards the future. For Tom, the future holds the promise of escape from the unbearable present, made all the more unbearable because of Amanda's recollection of the past. He is forced to listen to his mother reminisce about her past, and he does so without any real interest. The long monologues of his mother remain meaningless for him. When Tom Wingfield makes plans for the future, sadly that plan is accomplished with his abandonment of both the past and the present. For Laura, neither past, nor present, nor future connects her to the real world. Time seems to mean nothing to Laura, she remains imprisoned in the static present. Bluefarb feels that, in this play of time, time shows "three faces, each of these turned toward the tropism of its own fragmented vision" (517), and in this play, the conceptualisation of time gets tied to the trope of memory.

George Belliveau opines that both playwrights and performers make use of memory "to blur and to enlighten past and present events" (129). In memory plays, characters mull over moments from the past, re-evaluate themselves in that context, and simultaneously form a deeper understanding of the present. Belliveau further says that, as memory is viewed and performed through a theatrical lens, it is "literally embodied in the characters onstage, providing a unique vehicle for expression and understanding" (129).

Thus, faced with crisis, playwrights and the actors may use memory plays to recover from past trauma. Williams's *Menagerie* is one such play, perhaps one of the first plays to bring this genre to the forefront. In *Menagerie*, Tom Wingfield begins the play by directly addressing the audience, stating at the outset: "The play is memory. Being a memory play, it is dimly lighted, it is sentimental, it is not realistic" (5), and he proceeds to introduce them to his family members who appear in his memories. Tom therefore lives in two time zones, re-living in moments from the past and simultaneously existing in the present in front of the spectators. For Tom, then, the present bestows a rich context to understand the past events that occurred in his life.

In "The Catastrophe of Success", an introductory essay by Williams in the New Direction edition of *The Glass Menagerie*, the playwright says:

> It is only in his work that an artist can find reality and satisfaction, for the actual world is less intense than the world of his invention and consequently his life, without recourse to violent disorder, does not seem very substantial. The right condition for him is that in which his work is not only convenient but unavoidable.
>
> (102)

For the artist, as Shakespeare stated in *Hamlet*, the play *is* the thing. The play proves the artist's veracity. Williams tries to show this on stage with Tom Wingfield, the unusual artist who writes poems in the warehouse. This play is created and produced out of Tom's memory and, "memory and illusion become one with Tom as the artist" (Man 24). In fact, we do not really see Tom's mother and sister, but we do see Tom's memory of them. The depictions are filtered through Tom's perception. He speaks fondly of his sister, shows mixed feelings towards his mother, and also remembers not just their lives and the gentleman caller but also another member of the family – his father – the absent father whose memory hurts them very much. *The Glass Menagerie* by Williams and *Death of a Salesman* by Arthur Miller are pivoted around illusions which the characters indulge in – illusions which are bound to lead to eventual disillusionment of the characters as they confront reality. Glenn Man says that "in both plays, memory is employed as a device to precipitate and entertain the illusion. So what we have is the truth of human ideals and dreams acted out within the dream world of the stage" (23). Williams's plays keep on exaggerating human recklessness and indiscretions. One may complain that this is far from real life; yet, in spite of this sheer exaggeration, the plays of Williams manifest what is universal in human nature. Yet there are stark differences. In *Death of a Salesman*, the memory does not constitute the play, the memory is not the play. Memory is used merely as a technique to evoke Willy Loman's past dreams and that provides the trauma of failure, his failure to substantiate those dreams. In Williams's play, however, the memory technically is the play functioning concurrently to evoke the illusions of the characters, the Wingfields. As Thomas L. King states:

> Tom is the Prospero of *The Glass Menagerie*, and its world is the world of Tom's mind even more than *Death of a Salesman*'s is the world of Willy Loman's mind. … If Amanda looms large, she looms large in Tom's mind, not in her own right; though of course the image that finally dominates Tom's mind is that of Laura and the glass menagerie. (208)

Amanda keeps on living in the past and reminiscing about her gentleman callers in her youth. It is strange and pathetic that she keeps on clinging to this illusion, pathetic all the more because she tries to pass on this 'legacy' of past glory to her daughter. She keeps on attempting to bring her memories alive and recast them into the present. As a cripple, Laura shies away from accepting life as it is. The shy and withdrawn Laura, with a blank slate of a life, also indulges in her memories. As Man comments, in the case of Laura, "memory becomes present reality which, in turn, becomes memory again to effect the incarnation she stands for. Here memory functions not as a technicality but as theme" (27). Williams manages to bring to the forefront the memories of her high school days—probably the only period in her life with sweetness and beauty. At a significant moment in the play, one of her sweetest memories resurfaces, the memory of Jim O'Connor, her first crush, her one and only infatuation while she was in high school. The audience gets to know her memory of the name he had given her—Blue Roses—which actually arose out of an interesting miscommunication. She also remembers sitting through three of Jim's operatic performances so that she could obtain his autograph. She also has a rather painful memory of Jim's love for a girl who was far more attractive (or so Laura thought). To Laura, Jim O'Connor remained an illusion of a lover, someone like a movie star, an illusion which never became real for her. As Jim, the hero of her memories, re-enters her life in the present as the gentleman caller, memory becomes reality. This reality turns out to be a harsh one, however, as Jim brings up the issue of his engagement. So Laura is forced to go back to her world of memories and illusions. As Bluefarb mentions, for Laura, "it is neither past, present, nor future which holds the semblance of reality; nor does the past or future offer even the simulacrum of a make-believe reality" (517), adding that time has ceased to have any meaning whatever for Laura: "her whole existence turns on a fulcrum of no-time" (517). It may be claimed that none of the characters in *Menagerie* truly faces the flow of time. The Wingfields keep on looking for something that belongs to neither the past nor the present or the future, and the quest intersperses with the meanings of their half-lived and fragmented lives. At the end of the play, we find Tom having had escaped from this world of illusions that his mother and sister are denizens of. But he retains the memory of Laura, admitting that he will never be able to part with that. He says:

> … I was pursued by something. It always came upon me unawares, taking me altogether by surprise. … Then all at once my sister touches my shoulder, I turn around and look into her eyes. Oh Laura, Laura, I tried to leave you behind me, but I am more faithful than I intended to be!
> (97)

Thus, in *The Glass Menagerie*, it is Tom's memory that technically constitutes the whole play. As Tom utters these final words, the concepts of memory as theme and memory as technique become juxtaposed. As Tom takes his leave, the audience is left with Laura and Amanda and the blown-out candles. In the theatric retelling, Tom as actor and narrator looks back and contextualises the traumatic events in his past life. Eventually, he escapes, having used creative expression which becomes therapeutic; the objectivity and detachment of Tom the artist exorcise the pain as he creates the play.

Bibliography

Primary Text

Williams, Tennessee. *The Glass Menagerie*, edited by Stephen J. Bottoms, Methuen Drama India-Bloomsbury, 2015.

References

Belliveau, George. "Releasing Trauma." *Memory*, edited by Philippe Tortell et al., Peter Wall Institute for Advanced Studies, 2018, pp. 129–38. *JSTOR*, https://doi.org/10.2307/j.ctvbtzpfm.18. Accessed 5 Mar. 2024.

Bluefarb, Sam. "The Glass Menagerie: Three Visions of Time." *College English*, Vol. 24, No. 7, 1963, pp. 513–18. *JSTOR*, https://doi.org/10.2307/372877. Accessed 5 Mar. 2024.

Dela Cruz, Edgardo. "Things Loved; Things Remembered: Joaquin's 'Portrait' and Williams' 'Menagerie'." *Philippine Studies*, Vol. 14, No. 2, 1966, pp. 243–52. *JSTOR*, http://www.jstor.org/stable/42720097. Accessed 5 Mar. 2024.

King, Thomas L. "Irony and Distance in *The Glass Menagerie*." *Educational Theatre Journal*, Vol. 25, No. 2, 1973, pp. 207–14. *JSTOR*, https://doi.org/10.2307/3205871. Accessed 5 Mar. 2024.

Man, Glenn. "Memory as Technique and Theme in *The Glass Menagerie* and *The Death of a Salesman*." *Notre Dame English Journal*, Vol. 5, No. 2, 1970, pp. 23–30. *JSTOR*, http://www.jstor.org/stable/40066506. Accessed 5 Mar. 2024.

5 Experiments with Form in *The Glass Menagerie*

Adolphe Appia, a passionate Wagnerite, constantly trying to plan how Richard Wagner should be staged, emerged as a pioneer of modern staging. Though he was primarily a stage designer, he wrote on the theory of theatre. Lee Simonson, in an essay on Appia, says that Appia explained the theories and basic aesthetic principles of modern stage design in two volumes: *La Mise en Scéne du Drame Wagnérien* [*The Staging of Wagnerian Music-drama*] published in Paris in 1895, and *Die Musik und die Inscenierung* [*Music and Stage-Setting*] published in Munich in 1899. Simonson says that, to Appia, the aesthetic problem of scenic design was a plastic one. He adds, "The designer's task is to relate forms in space, some of which are static, some of which are mobile" (30), also mentioning that since the stage itself is an enclosed space, the organisation must be three-dimensional. Appia analysed four 'plastic' elements involved in scenic design: "perpendicular painted scenery, the horizontal floor, the moving actor, and the lighted space in which they are confined" (Simonson 30–31).

Frank Durham rightly states that the 20th-century audience wished to see life portrayed realistically and yet verse seemed to be absolutely artificial to them. Nevertheless, American dramatists began indulging in new forms of poetic drama, which eschewed verse "for an eclectic but organic union of both verbal and non-verbal elements of the theatre, which many critics have recognised and which Tennessee Williams, one of its major practitioners, calls 'plastic theatre'" (59–60). *Menagerie* is one of the finest examples of this form that Williams referred to as plastic theatre. American dramatists of this era were concerned with the performative aspects of theatre. Thus, 20th-century American poetic drama, as practised by Eugene O'Neill and Williams, turned out to be contemporary, maintaining full contact with reality and simultaneously seeking the essential emotional and psychic truths. As Alan Downer says:

> Thus the true poet of the theater is not necessarily concerned in the least with the traditional forms and language of poetry, but with

DOI: 10.4324/9781003504245-6

> making all the elements at his disposal — plot, actor, action, stage, lighting, setting, music, speech—unite to serve as a vehicle for his theme, his vision, or his interpretation of man's fate.

He adds:

> Properly handled, organically related to the action and purpose of the whole work, the devices of expressionism have permitted playwrights to penetrate beneath the surface of their situations, to reveal truths which realism by its nature tends to disguise. This penetration, this revelation of inner truth, brings the contemporary drama once more into a close relationship with the great repertory of the poetic drama of the past.
>
> (from *Fifty Years of American Drama, 1900–1950*, quoted in Durham 60)

In the "Author's Production Notes" to *The Glass Menagerie*, Williams mentions that he is attempting to indulge in this new form of poetic drama:

> Because of its considerably delicate or tenuous material, atmospheric touches and subtleties of direction play a particularly important part. Expressionism and all other unconventional techniques in drama have only one valid aim, and that is a closer approach to truth. When a play employs unconventional techniques, it is not, or certainly shouldn't be, trying to escape its responsibility of dealing with reality, or interpreting experience, but is actually or should be attempting to find a closer approach, a more penetrating and vivid expression of things as they are. The straight realistic play with its genuine frigidaire and authentic ice-cubes, its characters that speak exactly as the audience speaks, corresponds to the academic landscape and has the same virtue of photographic likeness. Everyone should know nowadays the unimportance of the photographic in art: that truth, life, or reality is an organic thing which the poetic imagination can represent or suggest, in essence, only through transformation, through changing into other forms than those which merely present an appearance.
>
> These remarks are not meant as a preface only to this particular play. They have to do with a conception of a new, plastic theatre which must take the place of the exhausted theatre of realistic conventions if the theatre is to resume vitality as a part of our culture.
>
> (quoted in Durham 61)

Williams's poetic drama and it's form thus turned out to be distinctly American, portraying the authenticity of American life and culture. Tom, his narrator in *The Glass Menagerie*, presents the spectator the "truth in the pleasant disguise of illusion" (4).

Williams and his contemporaries began experimenting with new forms as opposed to the traditional Aristotelian ones. Instead of the traditional form, they were dedicated instead, as Esther M. Jackson says, "to the creation of an anti-classical form which elevates lyric above story, spectacle above thought, and passion above reason" (9). To Williams, conventional American realistic theatre was dull and humdrum, and he wished to create a new kind of poetry on stage. As Stephen Bottoms mentions in his introduction, Williams came to the conclusion that he needed to seek "apocalypse without delirium" (lxiii), preferring muted understatement to loud and elaborate spectacle. Williams stated:

> I have evolved a new method which in my own particular case may turn out to be a solution. I call it the 'sculptural drama'.... I visualise it as a reduced mobility on stage the forming of statuesque attitudes on tableaux, something resembling a restrained type of dance, with motions honed down to only the essential or significant.
>
> (quoted in Bottoms lxiii)

The playwright's notebooks document his struggle to find a new methodology. The first thing that strikes us as we watch *Menagerie* is its simplicity. Keeping this simplicity intact, Williams presented the play as a series of episodes instead of adhering to the traditional three-act or five-act structure. As Bottoms says, *Menagerie* eventually evolved as a play with seven scenes, "each of which could serve to depict a distilled, 'sculptural' image of a situation, a relational dynamic between characters" (lxiii). Moreover, these scenes rarely have much of physical action, and the lack of action is compensated for by the sheer poetry of the characters' emotions. At the end of Scene Three, for example,

> *Tom is left with Laura. Laura clings weakly to the mantel with her face averted. Tom stares at her stupidly for a moment. Then he crosses to the shelf. He drops awkwardly on his knees to collect the fallen glass, glancing at Laura as if he would speak but couldn't.*
>
> (25)

Bottoms brings our attention to two more of Williams's stage directions that prevent the episodes from being dull and static. In Scene Five, as he describes Amanda and Laura, he writes,

> *Amanda and Laura are removing dishes from the table in the dining room, which is shadowy, their movements formalized almost as a dance or ritual, their moving forms as pale and silent as moths.*
>
> (38)

Again, at the end of Scene Seven, as the mother comforts her daughter,

> *Amanda's gestures are slow and graceful, almost dancelike, as she comforts her daughter.*
>
> (96)

The emotionally charged movements, the palpable stillness, and the deliberate silences and understatements add meaning to the sheer beauty of the innovative poetry on stage. Significant moments remain emotionally suffused yet subtle. Unlike those in conventional realistic drama, there is no 'rising action', yet the audience becomes acutely involved with the spectacle along with the restless emotions of the characters. Bottoms mentions that when *Menagerie* first appeared, the power of this play bewildered critics, the playwright having used a technique and a plot structure which seemed so simple and even uneventful. The *New York Herald Tribune* stated, "The lack of action in *The Glass Menagerie* is a bit baffling at first ... but it becomes of no consequence as one gets to know the family" (quoted in Bottoms lxiv). The audience gets to know the family as the play's muted stillness induces this intimacy with the Wingfields. In *Menagerie*, Williams discards conventional stage realism with a purpose to attain a sense of heightened and intensified emotional realism, which is achieved through the playwright's terse plot and 'sculptural' stillness.

The playwright defined *The Glass Menagerie* along with *Camino Real* and American Blues as plays of 'personal lyricism,' suggesting that his plays were vehicles of the expression of the self. In the later stages of his career, Williams developed another form, which, Jackson says, may be described as synthetic. It should be kept in mind that both of these concepts of form are not strictly realistic. *Menagerie* is a very fine example of Williams's early concept of form. As Gassner also mentions, the form of the play departs from the 'fourth wall' convention of realistic dramaturgy, and he finds similarities with "Japanese Noh-drama, in which story consists mostly of remembered fragments of experience" (391). At the outset, Tom the narrator says, "I am the opposite of a stage magician. He gives you the illusion that has the appearance of truth. I give you truth in the pleasant disguise of illusion" (4) and then boldly declares to the spectator that he is creating a theatrical illusion, as he says, "The play is memory" (5). This itself strips the play of what is traditionally termed 'action,' and therefore there is no traditional beginning, middle, or end. Tom takes up "three simultaneous identities: the 'I' as actor, the 'I' as creator and the 'I' as spectator. Through this figure, the dramatist invites the spectator to perceive a fragmentary vision, to recreate a momentary experience and to reflect upon a partial truth" (Jackson 14).As the play opens, right in the beginning, in his monologue in Scene One, Tom explains that since the play involves the evocation of his memories, it will be "dimly lighted" (5), and he further declares that the play "is sentimental, it is not realistic" (5) as it is a memory play. And as Williams had emphasised in his production notes, the lighting and music would not be mere accompaniments but integral parts of his play. As Bottoms mentions, his concern to create "a new, plastic theatre" meant that his would be "a theatre that provides a three-dimensional sensory experience, as opposed to being primarily verbal or literary" (lxvi). These new ideas were rather unusual in the 1940s, when Williams wrote this play, but they were responsible for the huge success of *Menagerie* and were very influential on other playwrights. Indeed, Williams used soul-stirring and poignant music, atmospheric lighting, and semi-transparent sets to create a new form of stage realism, evocative and almost dream-like. Interestingly, this was referred to for a while as 'the American Style,' a style that was first seen in *Menagerie* and then used in other plays such as *A Streetcar Named Desire*. This stage realism was subsequently adopted by other playwrights like Arthur Miller, who openly acknowledged the influence of Williams as he began to shape his own ideas for his landmark play *Death of a Salesman*.

Of all the stage devices that Williams used successfully, a prime one was the use of gauze scenery. Interestingly, when lit from the front, gauze scenery creates the illusion of a solid wall, but when lit from behind, it can almost vanish. As the stage directions show, Williams made an exhaustive use of gauze scenery in *Menagerie*; scenes behind the gauze appeared and dissolved, just as memories appear and dissolve in one's mind. Moreover, as Brenda Murphy says,

> Williams's use of the screen with 'legends' or title cards like those of silent film, along with the lighting, the music, and the other scenic elements, creates an aesthetic estrangement of the audience that keeps it from identifying with the characters, the *mise en scène*, and the action as if it were reality.
>
> (59)

According to Murphy, what made *The Glass Menagerie* "unique" as a play was its "overt presentation to the audience as a work of art, a play that made the subjective perception of memory into an aesthetic approach to truth" (59). Williams wrote in the production notes to *Menagerie*:

> expressionism and all other unconventional techniques in drama have only one valid aim, and that is a closer approach to truth. When a play employs unconventional techniques it is not, or certainly shouldn't be, trying to escape its responsibility of dealing with reality, or interpreting experience, but is actually or should be attempting to find a closer approach, a more penetrating and vivid expression of things as they are.
>
> (quoted in Murphy 59)

Legendary American theatrical scenic and lighting designer Jo Mielziner, referred to as the most successful set designer of the Golden era of Broadway, worked on the premiere productions of most of Williams's and Miller's famous plays. Mielziner had carved a niche for himself with his innovative designs for plays such as *Street Scene* (1929) and *Ethan Frome* (1936). In fact, it was his association with playwrights Williams and Miller and director Elia Kazan that led to a form of total theatre that would be recognised worldwide as 'the American style,' a theatre form that would become very influential too.

Following Williams's production notes for *Menagerie*, Mielziner for the first time attempted an aesthetic which he would express in scenic terms as "abstract realism." This was "an aesthetic that suggested the artist's subjective intervention in the illusion of reality without moving entirely into a subjective vision, as expressionism does" (Murphy 59). As the first scene opened, Tom entered the stage and stood on a fire escape in front of the brick wall of the house. What the audience actually saw was a canvas wall with a scrim, which is a piece of gauze cloth that appears opaque until lit from behind. In front of the scrim came the present time, namely the time in which Tom began narrating the play. This is how the playwright presented the audience with objective reality, something that the audience shared with Tom. Then began Tom's monologue. As he finished his monologue, there appeared a dim blue light. The interior of the apartment was revealed through the scrim lit from behind with blue light. This was a visual representation of how the audience entered into Tom's memory as he in turn began to narrate what became the play's action with Amanda and Laura. The set consisted primarily of a living room, and upstage was an opening with portieres or curtains, also gauze, which divided the living room from the dining room. The figures in the dining room would first be seen faintly, as if they were appearing through layers of memory. Thomas Scheye stated, "the portieres curtain off an inner stage; they are another dividing line between illusion and reality or one kind of truth and another" (quoted in Murphy 61). Such was the set designing that the dining room portieres opened after Amanda's first speech and also after Tom entered the scene with Amanda and Laura; the whole scrim structure representing the outer wall of the apartment building rose up into the wings as the play's (past) action began, and it descended as Tom left at the end of the play, once again coming to represent the screen of memory through which he presents his sister and mother.

Williams's use of magic lanterns was also remarkable. The magic lanterns or the slide projections produced hazy, flexible, and plastic images. Williams underscored a series of titles and images. The hazy unfixed images suggested the playwright's attempt to portray the fuzzy and nebulous world of dreams. The first projection, in Scene One, is 'Ou son les neiges' (6). This is a segment of a line by French poet François Villon: 'Ou sont les neiges d'antan?', which means 'Where are the snows of yesteryear?' The words are evocative of past memories, emotions, and nostalgia. In Scene Two, the Screen image is that of blue roses. As blue roses do not exist in reality, the screen triggers certain questions in the minds of the spectators. Much later, the audience learns that Blue Roses was Jim's nickname for Laura when they were in high school. Bottoms says, "Williams thus creates a strange, elliptical link between present and past moments, looping backwards in time rather than obeying the usual, logical linearity of dramatic narrative" (lxx). Williams continues doing this throughout the play; the slide projections are all subtly suggestive and resonant rather than specific and defined. Titles used on the slide projections also remain suggestive, sometimes acting as ironic commentaries; for example, when Jim informs the family that he is going steady with Betty, his girlfriend and fiancée, a caption appears that reads '*the sky falls*,' (93) which obviously sums up the mother's stunned reaction.

With his acute interest in innovative lighting and translucent scenery Mielziner turned out to be the ideal designer to work with. In his memoir *Designing for the Theatre*, Mielziner wrote that "if Tennessee Williams had written plays in the days before the technical development of translucent and transparent scenery, I believe he would have invented it" (quoted in Murphy 60). Mielziner enhanced Williams's inventive ideas, stating that his

> use of translucent and transparent scenic interior walls was not just another trick. It was a true reflection of the contemporary playwright's interest in–and at times obsession with–the exploration of the inner man. Williams was writing not only a memory play but a play of influences that were not confined within the walls of a room.
>
> (quoted in Murphy 60)

Bottoms reminds us that the phrase used by Mielziner, 'the inner man,' was a familiar one among artists of the first half of the 20th century because of the emergence of the modernist movement of expressionism. Williams was definitely exposed to expressionism, and in his production notes for *Menagerie*, he refers to "expressionism and all other unconventional techniques in drama" as helping inspire his concern to create a "new plastic theatre" (quoted in Bottoms lxvii). Bottoms adds that "*Menagerie* itself can be seen as expressionist insofar that it explores Tom's inner turmoil by depicting his memories — obviously an 'expression' of his inner mind — with the help of appropriately 'dreamlike' lighting and sound" (Bottoms lxvii). The nostalgic yearning and the misty bleary memories viewed through the scrims were far from being expressionistic, however. Moreover, Williams repeatedly uses a kind of split-focus effect, along with certain cinematic effects, drawing the audience's attention simultaneously in two directions, giving the audience the opportunity of choosing what to look at. David Savran points out that this too is antithetical to expressionism, adding that this method has more affinity with surrealism. In *The Surrealist Manifesto*, published in 1924, poet and critic André Breton stated that surrealism was a means of reuniting conscious and subconscious ambits of experience wholly so that the worlds of dream and fantasy would be fused with the everyday rational world in an absolute reality, a surreality. Thus, it is evident that Williams's *Menagerie*, though influenced by expressionism, was definitely not an expressionistic play and was also not blatantly realistic but surrealistic. Williams's use of magic lantern slides underscores his use of split focus, as the audience's attention gets diverted from the characters and actors to the slide projections. The captions and images on the translucent slides also enhance Williams's surrealism. Bottoms mentions that in a production of his own in 1999, he chose to do away with magic lanterns, choosing "modern video technology to create fluid, dream-like image sequences inspired by Williams' suggestions" (lxxi). Indeed, if directors adopt this method now, it would not be discordant with Williams's original stage directions and suggestions since he used quite a few ideas and methods inspired by cinema.

George W. Crandell elucidates how Tom's vision and his recollection of family events in *The Glass Menagerie* "are both a reflection of the shaping influence of the cinema and, more importantly, an articulation of the dominant cultural ideology as expressed by the cinematic apparatus" (1). Williams's biographers have said much about the acquisition of knowledge regarding cinema and cinematic techniques because of his brief stint in 1943 at MGM, but Allean Hale reminds us that he acquired this knowledge already during his adolescence which he had spent in St. Louis, a city that "had more motion picture theatres per capita than New York City," adding that he "had spent twenty years at the movies before he went to Hollywood" (610). Indeed, Williams learnt much from cinema and amongst his plays, *Menagerie* is one which is extremely cinematic in form.

The opening scene has Amanda and Laura seated in the dining room at the rear end of the living room. The scene commences with what is referred to as a 'long shot' in movies. The two women are seen through a pair of scrim curtains; this produces the effect of unreality and distance. As the scrim representing the outside wall is raised, Tom the narrator joins his mother and sister. Then Williams directs the raising of the inner scrim, and the effect becomes akin to the camera taking a closer shot. Williams called for subtitles and images to be projected on a section of the wall between the front-room and the dining-room—just as the directors did in the silent films. As Durham mentions, in silent films, "a subtitle was often used at the beginning of a scene to tell the audience what to expect, sometimes to give the mood or thematic significance of the images to follow" (64). When Laura and Amanda are revealed, the subtitle is 'Ou son les neiges' (6), as mentioned already. Williams says that the screen device was originally intended:

> to give accent to certain values in each scene. Each scene contains a particular point (or several) which is structurally most important. In an episodic play, such as this, the basic structure or narrative line may be obscured from the audience; the effect may seem fragmentary rather than architectural.... The legend or image upon the screen will strengthen the effect of what is merely allusion in the writing and allow the primary point to be made more simply and lightly than if the entire responsibility were on the spoken lines.
>
> (quoted in Durham 64)

This structure, much used in the silent films, which had a series of short scenes, each one with a certain detail, with little or no transition in between, led to a cumulative effect, and this is referred to as a montage in cinematic language, originally associated with the works of D.W. Griffith and Sergei Eisenstein. In fact, in his comments on lighting and in his use of it in the play, Williams frequently suggests cinematic camera shots. He employs light, for example, for reaction close-ups. He says:

> Shafts of light are focused on selected areas or actors, sometimes in contradistinction to what is the apparent centre. For instance in the quarrel scene between Tom and Amanda, in which Laura has no active part, the clearest pool of light is on her figure. This is also true of the supper scene, when her silent figure on the sofa should remain the visual centre.
>
> (quoted in Durham 64)

In this way, Williams emphasised not just the actions of the character but the character's reaction to that action, and he highlighted the character's actions as they are highlighted in cinema with the use of the close-up shots. His use of diffused lighting is reminiscent of the kind Griffith used to employ. For example, Williams calls for a special lighting on Laura: "The light upon Laura should be distinct from the others, having a peculiar pristine clarity such as the light used in early religious portraits of female saints or madonnas," which underscores her fragility. He further instructs that, throughout the production, the light should resemble the light in religious art, especially the paintings of El Greco. The lighting is such that it brings to prominence the absent father in his photograph.

In Scene 3, when he shows Amanda trying to sell magazine subscriptions on the telephone,

> *She is spotlighted in the dim stage* (20).

Here he makes use of the cinematic close-up. As the rest of the stage remains dark, Amanda stands alone in a circle of light. Similarly, mother and son begin quarrelling behind the portières, and:

> *In front of them stands Laura with clenched hands and panicky expression. A clear pool of light on her figure throughout this scene* (20).

These close-up shots give way to long shots of the entire room. In the whole play, Williams says a "free, imaginative use of light can be of enormous value in giving a mobile plastic quality to plays of a more or less static nature".

Analysing the effects of cinema even more thoroughly, Crandell mentions the "cinematic role" and the "distinctive gaze" (2) of the narrator Tom Wingfield. To Crandell, *Menagerie* replicates what he calls "the organizational structures of the classic cinema" (2), which, in turn, reflect the ideology of a society which is patriarchal. Tom functions almost as a camera in a movie picture, providing the spectator with what Crandell refers to as "an orienting point of view" (3), coercing the spectator to identify with that point of view. Functioning as a camera, Tom is the 'eye,' and as the first-person narrator, Tom is the 'I' narrator. Crandell mentions another cinematic technique, "the shot-to-shot or shot/reverse shot formation" (4). Explaining this shot/reverse shot technique, Kaja Silverman states in *The Subject of Semiotics*:

> The shot/reverse shot formation is a cinematic set in which the second shot shows the field from which the first shot is assumed to have been taken.... [T]he viewing subject, unable to sustain for long its belief in the autonomy of the cinematic image, demands to know whose gaze controls what it sees. The shot/reverse shot formation is calculated to answer that question in such a manner that the cinematic illusion remains intact: Shot 1 shows a space which may or may not contain a human figure (e.g. the wall of a building, a view of the ocean, a room full of people).... Shot 2 locates a spectator in the other 180° of the same circular field, thereby implying that the preceding shot was seen through the eyes of a figure in the cinematic narrative.
>
> (quoted in Crandell 4)

In Shot 1, then, in *Menagerie*, the audience first observes the apartment of the Wingfields. Shot 2 is seen through the eyes of the 'I' narrator Tom, whose gaze controls the women he remembers in what he introduces as "a memory play" (5). Tom functions as and controls them as an omniscient narrator too, describing events and conversations between his mother and sister which he had not witnessed. In the shot/reverse shot technique, the spectator alternately becomes the subject and object of the look or gaze. As Williams replicates the technique of shot and reverse shot in *Menagerie*, he also replicates the technique of the suture.

The suture technique in films refers to the process by which we are drawn into the fictional world created by the moviemakers. Literally, the word refers to surgical stitching where the lips of a cut or incision are stitched together. In psychoanalytic film theory, suture serves as a metaphor for the 'stitching' of a spectator into the narrative illusion, primarily through the use of the shot/reverse shot technique. Jacques-Alain Miller says that suture may be defined as "the relation of the subject to the chain of its discourse" (quoted in Crandell 6). A successful application of the technique of suture makes the audience forget that they have been drawn into an imaginary world with the help of the camera eye or lens; the audience gets absorbed into the action and gets lost in the story/narrative. It is natural that narratives need to sew up discontinuities, namely transitions in terms of time and/or place, changeover from one consciousness to another, and switching from one plot line to another. In the 1960s, after a rereading of Freud's writings on the unconscious, Jacques Lacan offered a psychoanalytical explanation of how a subject is tied to discourse by its need to suture over gaps constantly opening up between it and its representation in discourse. In 1969, this Lacanian concept of suture was applied to the nature of cinematic narrative.

In *Menagerie*, Tom Wingfield not just defines but also controls the point of view of the spectator. Kaja Silverman, in "Dis-Embodying the Female Voice", observes that Hollywood 'classic' cinema abounds in shot/reverse shot formations in which men look at women; in other words, it is "axiomatic that the female subject is the object rather than the subject of the gaze in mainstream narrative cinema … she functions as an organizing spectacle, as the lack which structures the symbolic order and sustains the relay of male glances" (131). In *Menagerie*, the two women in Tom Wingfield's life—his mother Amanda and his sister Laura—become objects of his gaze. Silverman also mentions that the female protagonist is often employed as a signifier of castration or lack. In keeping with the organisational pattern typical of the 'classic cinema,' roles are assigned as in patriarchal society where, as Laura Mulvey explains, there is "[a]n active/passive heterosexual division of labour" where "the man's role [is] the active one of forwarding the story, [of] making things happen" (quoted in Crandell 7). In *Menagerie*, Tom indeed makes things happen as the plot pivots around his trying to secure for his sister a gentleman caller who will eventually become her husband and fill up the lack. In fact, in *Menagerie*, Tom constantly underscores the lack of a husband not just for his sister but also for his mother. Amanda Wingfield's constant presence almost fades away because of the formidable presence of the large portrait of Mr. Wingfield, who had abandoned them long back. Silverman says that it is equally axiomatic that the female subject in Hollywood movies is denied any active role in discourse. She says in "Dis-Embodying the Female Voice":

> Like the male subject, the female subject emerges only within discourse … However, whereas the male subject has privileges conferred upon him by his relationship to discourse, the female subject is defined as insufficient through hers.
>
> … [T]he male subject is granted access to what Foucault calls 'discursive fellowships,' …In other words, he is allowed to occupy the position of the speaking subject—in fiction, and even to some degree in fact. Within dominant narrative cinema the male subject enjoys not only specular but linguistic authority.
>
> The female subject, on the contrary, is associated with unreliable, thwarted, or acquiescent speech. She talks a great deal; it would be a serious mistake to characterize her as silent, since it is in large part through her prattle, her bitchiness, her sweet murmurings, her maternal admonitions, and her verbal cunning that we know her.
>
> (131–132)

This perfectly sums up the situation Amanda finds herself in. In spite of her discursive presence, Amanda lacks authority. It is Tom, who is the figure of authority in the play, who clearly resembles what Laura Mulvey describes as the typical male protagonist in films, a "controlling figure with whom the spectator can identify" (quoted in Crandell 7).

In accordance with the way patriarchy operates, men have an active role in movies, and women passive ones. As Tom gazes at his mother and sister, they react differently to it. Amanda accepts her role as the object of a man's attention, reminiscing over her gentlemen callers and also becoming an exhibitionist as Jim O'Connor, intended to be the gentleman caller for her daughter, pays them a visit. She proudly announces, "I'm going to make a spectacular appearance!" (53). Amanda hopes that Laura will also try to appear attractive to men and thereby get herself a husband—a provider and protector. In fact, she stuffs Laura's flat chest with powder puffs in order to add some sex appeal. Laura, however, actively keeps on resisting the role prescribed for women in patriarchal society despite her mother Amanda's insistence that she conform to it. She resists the male gaze in *Menagerie*, both her brother's and Jim's. Laura's character is an alternative to the conventional role of the woman in a patriarchal society. She offers resistance, representing what Silverman, in *The Subject of Semiotics*, describes as "the temptation to refuse cultural re-integration, to skid off-course, out of control, to prefer castration to false plentitude" (quoted in Crandell 9).

These techniques that Williams adopts from the cinema—long shot, montage, the shot/reverse shot leading to the suture, and the patriarchal gaze—serve as techniques which control the audience's response.

Bibliography

Primary Text

Williams, Tennessee. *The Glass Menagerie*, edited by Stephen J. Bottoms, Methuen Drama India-Bloomsbury, 2015.

References

Crandell, George W. "The Cinematic Eye in Tennessee Williams's *The Glass Menagerie*." *The Tennessee Williams Annual Review*, No. 1, 1998, pp. 1–11. *JSTOR*, https://doi.org/10.2307/45343903. Accessed 6 Mar. 2024.

Durham, Frank. "Tennessee Williams, Theatre Poet in Prose." *Modern Critical Interpretations: Tennessee Williams's The Glass Menagerie*, edited and with an introduction by Harold Bloom, Chelsea House Publishers, 1988, pp. 59–73.

Gassner, John. "Tennessee Williams: Dramatist of Frustration." *The English Journal*, Vol. 37, No. 8, 1948, pp. 387–93. *JSTOR*, https://doi.org/10.2307/807030. Accessed 5 Mar. 2024.

Hale, Allean. "Tennessee Williams's St. Louis Blues." *The Mississippi Quarterly*, Vol. 48, No. 4, 1995, pp. 609–25. *JSTOR*, http://www.jstor.org/stable/26475759. Accessed 5 Mar. 2024.

Jackson, Esther M. "The Problem of Form in the Drama of Tennessee Williams." *CLA Journal*, Vol. 4, No. 1, 1960, pp. 8–21. *JSTOR*, http://www.jstor.org/stable/44327928. Accessed 5 Mar. 2024.

Murphy, Brenda. *The Theatre of Tennessee Williams (Critical Companions)*. Bloomsbury, 2014.

Silverman, Kaja. "Dis-Embodying the Female Voice". *Re-vision: Essays in Feminist Film Criticism*, edited by Doane, Mary Ann, et al., University Publications of America, 1984, pp. 131–49.

Simonson, Lee. "The Ideas of Adolphe Appia." *The Theory of the Modern Stage: An Introduction to Modern Theatre and Drama*, edited by Eric Bentley, Penguin, 1968, pp. 27–50.

6 The Wingfields and the Gentleman Caller

A Study of the Characters in *The Glass Menagerie*

In one's study of the characters in *The Glass Menagerie*, one might begin by asking how many characters the play presents us with. One could say there are the Wingfields and Jim O'Connor, the gentleman caller; one could also say that there is only one character in the play: Tom Wingfield. Though Amanda is a formidable character and though the glass menagerie belongs to Laura, the play belongs to Tom. Tom opens the play and also closes it; Amanda, Laura, and the gentleman caller do appear in the play, but the audience sees not the characters but Tom's memory of them. In a study of the major plays of Tennessee Williams, Desmond Reid states that the people which he presents the audience with are people in distress, usually "people in desperate trouble: they are lonely, forgotten, poverty-stricken, misunderstood or despised, without hope of helping themselves and unhelped by others" (432). He adds that Williams stays remarkably faithful to himself and his theme and that sometimes he "crowds all the trouble on to the shoulders of one unhappy person; sometimes there are two or three, equally unhappy, whose lives and troubles intermingle; sometimes he leaves them at the curtain-fall with a dim ray of hope; more often there is none" (432). This description would very well befit the Wingfields in *Menagerie*; each one is troubled, lonely, frustrated, and desperate. The play, set in the troubled 1940s, deals with the profound loss that each character experiences.

Mr. Wingfield: The Absent Father

Paul Nagim Rosefeldt states that one way to understand how modern drama plays out profound loss "for that which once was or, at least, was thought to be, is to explore the workings of the absent father in modern plays" (3). The absent father is the father who is central to the dramatic action but who does not ever appear on the stage. Drama ideally should focus on present action in which the events should be shown, not narrated to an audience. Peter Szondi defines drama as "always primary; its internal

DOI: 10.4324/9781003504245-7

time is always the present. … In the drama, time unfolds as an absolute linear sequence in the present" (quoted in Rosefeldt 4). However, *Menagerie*, placing Tom as the narrator protagonist, brings diegesis to the forefront and emphasises a dramaturgy where actions are not presented but represented and mediated through his discourse. Thus, as this play unfolds, it begins to recapture much that has been lost.

Mr. Wingfield, the absent father, is introduced by his son, Tom, as "the fifth character in the play" (5). Rosefeldt speaks about the characteristic features of the absent characters in plays. He says that they may exist in past time, namely a time prior to the action of the play, or they may exist in the present time but be spatially removed from the action of the play. Absent characters are often represented by iconic markers such as photographs or metonymic signs—in *Menagerie*, the stage direction mentions "*A blown-up photograph of the father hangs on the wall of the living room*" (4). The actions and physical characteristics of the absent character may be recounted in the discourse of other characters—indeed, Amanda and Tom constantly recount the actions and good looks of Mr. Wingfield—and, obviously, as the actions are recounted, they also become filtered through the point of view of someone else. Naturally, as the absent character is constantly reconstructed in various dimensions of the text, he has the scope neither to explain his or her actions nor to contradict the representation that others construct. Rosefeldt writes:

> The absent character, thus, becomes a syphon and a magnet, an Other that becomes reflected and refracted throughout the dramatic environment. By its very nature, the absent character maintains a liminal space between absence and presence and is both outside (not in the plot) and inside (in the story) of the drama. Often when focal to the play, such a character can take on symbolic significance.
>
> (7)

Drama being an art form where characters have to be present in person on stage, the absent character cannot ever appear in person, yet he exists in the discourse of others or is represented, always removed from the present action. Rosefeldt calls the absent character a liminal figure, "halfway between being missing and present, life and death, past and present, the 'what was' and 'the never will be,' a presence that is always being deferred" (9). In the modernist plays of the absent father, Rosefeldt finds a distinct pattern. The father who is absent from the family is either dead or has abandoned his children. He becomes a mysterious figure, "connected to the family, yet outside of the family, a representative of the values of his culture, yet a transgressor of those values" (22).

In the Williams household, father and son did not like each other. Edwina Dakin Williams stated in her book, "He took no joy in the children … The most trivial act might spin him into a tantrum" (quoted in Fritscher 7). And this is what Williams also recounted about his own father: "Often the voice of my father … was harsh. And sometimes it sounded like thunder. He was a big man.… And it was not a benign bigness. You wanted to shrink from it, to hide yourself" (quoted in Fritscher 7). In other plays of Williams, the father has a commanding presence. In *Cat on a Hot Tin Roof*, Williams portrays a bullying heartless father; Alma's father in *Summer and Smoke* is portrayed as a religious fanatic; in *Sweet Bird of Youth*, Heavenly's powerful father is determined to make Chance, a gigolo, pay for the injury, and Chance fears being attacked by Heavenly's father and then presumably being castrated. *Menagerie* portrays an absent father who remains an imposing figure even after he has left.

Mr. Wingfield, the absent father who abandoned his family years back, is not given a first name in the play. He is shown to be a solipsistic individual and a fugitive, "a telephone man who fell in love with long distances" (5), in a state of incessant flight as his postcard manifests. The postcard (not even a letter) just says, "Hello—Goodbye" (5). Yet remnants of the solipsistic individual are strewn everywhere in the Wingfield household. As Tom says, his gallant smile seems to be saying, "*I will be smiling forever*" (4). His daughter Laura keeps on "eternally play[ing] those worn out phonograph records [her] father left as a painful reminder of him" (16). After all those years, Amanda Wingfield, his wife, still wears his huge bathrobe "as a relic of the faithless Mr. Wingfield" (22). This is a painful reminder that Amanda's life has come to a standstill from the time Mr. Wingfield left. She keeps on recreating the past via nostalgic remembrance of her life before the disappearance of her husband and coerces her children into idealising their father. In fact, Amanda goes back in her mind to the moment when she fell in love with Mr. Wingfield. She reminiscences: "Malaria fever and jonquils and then—this—boy…." (54). Her use of the word 'boy' implies an ever-youthful paradise. In her remembrances, the young Mr. Wingfield, the charmer, comes from an idyllic world of "gracious living" (64). Amanda remembers that, when he smiled, "the world was *enchanted*" (46). The play constantly reminds us that Wingfield was never really part of the Southern agrarian aristocracy that Amanda cherishes; he, as a telephone man, consciously had chosen to be part of the world of modern technology instead. Amanda's idolizing is coupled with Tom's transformation of his father into a figure almost mythical. Mr. Wingfield's picture shows "*a very handsome young man in a doughboy's First World War cap*" (4), and Tom sees and idolizes his father as a soldier of fortune. Indeed, Mr. Wingfield heads westward, taking the direction of the mythic and legendary American heroes. The fugitive husband and father always remains out of reach and leaves "no address" (5) for his family. As Amanda tells Jim O'Connor, "Now he travels and I don't even know where!" (64). No one comes to know what eventually happens to him; Mr. Wingfield's travelling, vague and undisclosed, remains a mystery.

Amanda Wingfield

In most productions of *The Glass Menagerie*, which actress is playing Amanda becomes important; and Amanda is usually played by a powerful actress. The first production had Laurette Taylor, and over the years, as documented by Stephen Bottoms, Amanda has been played by Helen Hayes (New York, 1956), Maureen Stapleton (New York, 1965 and 1975), Jessica Tandy (New York, 1983), Susannah York (London, 1989), Julie Harris (New York, 1994), Zoe Wanamaker (London, 1995), and Sally Field (New York, 2017) (*Handbook* 58–59, 72).

Clearly based on his mother, Edwina Dakin Williams, Amanda Wingfield has been portrayed by Williams as a complex human being—a formidable character, a domineering mother. In *The Reproduction of Mothering*, Nancy Chodorow begins by stating:

> Women mother. In our society, as in most societies, women not only bear children. They also take primary responsibility for infant care, spend more time with infants and children than do men, and sustain primary emotional ties with infants. … Though fathers and other men spend varying amounts of time with infants and children, the father is rarely a child's primary parent.
>
> (3)

Chodorow makes a thorough social analysis of the way the ideology of mothering has evolved over the last two centuries, saying that the role of the family diminished in terms of material production; the family also lost much of its educational and religious role and its role in the care of the sick and aged. She adds that the family "became a quintessentially relational and personal institution, *the* personal sphere of society. Women's family role became centered on child care and taking care of men" (4–5). This aspect of taking care became intensified in 'nuclear' Western families which usually contained a married couple with children. Chodorow mentions how capitalist industrialisation removed from the household grown children, grandparents, and non-family members and "sharply curtailed men's participation in family life" (5). This in turn led to women's mothering becoming more isolated and absolute, with or without participation in the paid labour force, and infant and child care becoming an exclusive domain of biological mothers, who became increasingly isolated from other kin and with little social contacts. The mothering role, says Chodorow, involved more than physical labour. It was "relational and personal and, in the case of both children and men, maternal" (5). Amanda is shown in a somewhat pathetic light; at the outset, her son mentions how her husband "who doesn't appear except in [a] larger-than-life-size photograph" (5) abandoned her. Tom says, "This is our father who left us a long time ago. He was a telephone man who fell in love with long distances" (5). Amanda Wingfield fits in with the ideology of the 'moral mother' which Chodorow rightly opines was produced during the early capitalist period in America. In accordance with this ideology, bourgeois women were supposed to be nurturant moral models to their children as well as nurturant supporters and moral guides for their husbands; along with providing the husband with food and a clean house, a wife ideally had to be her husband's holy haven as he returned from the outside, immoral competitive world of work. Though this ideology lost some of its Victorian rigidity, it remained nevertheless and spread throughout society. Chodorow says, "women's mothering role has gained psychological and ideological significance, and has come increasingly to define women's lives" (4). The Wingfield family being one with an absent father and having been one with an emotionally remote father when Mr. Wingfield was around, Amanda's attentions and moral guidance get focussed entirely around her children, a situation which leads to violent clashes with her son. What strikes the audience first in *The Glass Menagerie* is the strained mother–son relationship. The worst clashes are those between mother and son. Right in the opening scene, Amanda instructs her son about good table manners as one would instruct a small child:

AMANDA [to her son]: Honey, don't *push* with your *fingers*. If you have to push with something, the thing to push with is a crust of bread. And chew—chew! Animals have secretions in their stomachs which enable them to digest flood without mastication, but human beings are supposed to chew their food before they swallow it down. Eat food leisurely, son, and really enjoy it. A well-cooked meal has lots of delicate flavours that have to be held in the mouth for appreciation. So chew your food and give your salivary glands a chance to function!

[*Tom deliberately lays his imaginary fork down and pushes his chair back from the table.*]

TOM: I haven't enjoyed one bite of this dinner because of your constant directions on how to eat it. It's you that makes me rush through meals with your hawklike attention to every bite I take. Sickening—spoils my appetite—all this discussion of— animals' secretion—salivary glands—mastication !

(6)

Tom does not only object to his mother's criticism of his table manners, he keeps on repeating many of her expressions to prove how much he hates to be criticised as an adult male. Soon we have Laura's gentle acceptance of her mother's familiar reminiscence of her gentlemen callers, a habit that the audience soon understands:

TOM: I know what's coming
LAURA: Yes. But let her tell it.
TOM: Again?
LAURA: She loves to tell it.

(7)

Just a few minutes after his violent reaction to his mother's criticism, he comes up with a sarcastic response to Amanda's gentlemen callers, unlike Laura:

AMANDA: One Sunday afternoon in Blue Mountain—your mother received—*seventeen*! gentlemen callers! Why, sometimes there weren't chairs enough to accommodate them all. We had to send the nigger over to bring in folding chairs from the parish house.
TOM [remaining at the portières]: How did you entertain those gentleman callers?
AMANDA: I understood the art of conversation!
TOM: I bet you could talk.
AMANDA: Girls in those days *knew* how to talk, I can tell you.
TOM: Yes?

(8)

There are violent clashes again in Scene Three. The mother and son, both headstrong, constantly try to silence one another, each one trying to prove the other wrong. Amanda continues to reprimand the twenty-three-year-old son as one would reprimand a teenager. She criticises his language, his expressions, his tastes, and his manners. Her moral mothering leads her to interfere in his indulgence in reading adult fiction, by D.H. Lawrence, which by her moral standards is no more than 'filth.'

TOM: What in Christ's name am I—
AMANDA [shrilly]: Don't you use that—

TOM:	—supposed to do!
AMANDA:	—expression! Not in my —
TOM:	Ohhh!
AMANDA:	—presence! Have you gone out of your senses?
AMANDA:	What is the matter with you, you —big— big—IDIOT !
TOM:	Look !—I've got *no thing*, no single thing—
AMANDA:	Lower your voice !
TOM:	—in my life here that I can call my OWN! Everything is—
AMANDA:	Stop that shouting !
TOM:	Yesterday you confiscated my books! You had the nerve to—
AMANDA:	I took that horrible novel back to the library—yes! That hideous book by that insane Mr. Lawrence.

...

BUT I WON'T ALLOW SUCH FILTH BROUGHT INTO MY HOUSE! No, no, no, no, no!

...

TOM:	I don't want to hear any more!
	...
AMANDA:	You will hear more, you—
TOM:	No, I won't hear more, I'm going out!
AMANDA:	You come right back in—
TOM:	Out, out, out! Because I'm—
AMANDA:	Come back here, Tom Wingfield! I'm not through talking to you!
TOM:	Oh, go—
LAURA [desperately]:	—Tom!
AMANDA:	You're going to listen, and no more insolence from you! I'm at the end of my patience!

(20–22)

Sometimes, the Wingfields become uncouth and direct in their futile efforts to silence one another; after this quarrel quoted above, Tom calls Amanda an "ugly—babbling old—*witch*..." (24). Amanda's actions could very well be representations of moral mothering, or there could be another interpretation of these clashes. In his analysis of modern plays with the absent father, Rosefeldt says that, in such plays, the mother is often represented as "the 'crazy' mother or the Terrible Mother who ignores, persecutes or betrays her children" (22–23).

In his notes on the characters, Williams describes Amanda as a "little woman of great but confused vitality clinging frantically to another time and place .... She is not paranoiac, but her life is paranoia." It is this living in 'another time and place' and her total obliviousness to the present that lead to her maladjustment with her children. As Sam Bluefarb says, "Amanda Wingfield, the mother, lives in a world that is emotionally bounded by the past. Although she quite literally inhabits the present, she is incapable of inhabiting that present other than in terms of her past" (513). Her splendid past life as a happy and ebullient Southern belle is constantly kept alive in her memory. She keeps on recalling words and gestures related to every event worth remembering, events involving gentlemen callers, on one occasion as many as seventeen. Bluefarb writes that, in order to "facilitate her periodic resurrections of the past, Amanda engages in a kind of dramatic monologue, in which she not only reports on past events, but on what transpired in the way of who said what to whom" (513–514). Amanda eagerly wants people, especially her children, to listen to her reminiscences, to her memories which contain facts albeit seen through rose-coloured lenses. She keeps on digging into her strata of memories, which her children are forced to listen to. She refuses to accept the present and, what is worse, refuses to accept what is true, and that includes her daughter's lameness. Unfortunately, Amanda fails to extricate herself from the past and associate herself with the present and fails also to comprehend how much of a misfit her children will be in the present times if they model themselves after her and follow her instructions. Tom openly manifests a disgust towards these long self-aggrandising speeches which Amanda indulges in; and Laura listens to her mother patiently but without real interest and even tries to hold back her brother from reacting sharply and aggressively to them. As both her daughter and her son remain quiet when she talks, the effect of her words on the audience becomes akin to a monologue. Though Tom's escape is referred to as a romantic escape, it is not Tom but Amanda who is a true romantic, a person obsessed with the past and a person remote from the present realities.

Chodorow mentions that psychoanalytic accounts presuppose that good and desirable maternal care will "arise from the mothers' 'empathy' with her infant and her treatment of it as an extension of herself—as someone whose interests she knows through total regressive identification, or as someone whose interests are absolutely identical with her own" (82). Instead of trying to understand her children's interests, Amanda not only remains acutely immersed in the past but she also becomes obsessed with superimposing her own past on her daughter's future. She sees Laura as an extension of her younger self, not as an individual, and wants her to have all that she possessed—good looks, charm, beautiful dresses, the balls in the aristocratic South, and, of course, gentlemen callers—refusing to admit what is true and real and present, as manifested in this conversation:

AMANDA:	Girls that aren't cut out for business careers usually wind up married to some nice man. [*She gets up with a spark of revival.*] Sister, that's what you'll do!

[*LAURA utters a startled, doubtful laugh. She reaches quickly for a piece of glass.*]

LAURA:	But, Mother—
AMANDA:	Yes ? [*She goes over to the photograph.*]
LAURA [in a tone of frightened apology]:	I'm—crippled!
AMANDA:	Nonsense! Laura, I've told you never, never to use that word. Why, you're not crippled, you just have a little defect—hardly noticeable, even! When people have some slight disadvantage like that, they cultivate other things to make up for it—develop charm—and vivacity—and—*charm*! That's all you have to do! ...

(17–18)

Remembering her numerous gentlemen callers, including her husband, she wants such a gentleman caller to appear and ask for the hand of her daughter. She remains tied to the rose-coloured past, but as evident in her reminiscences, she keeps worrying for her daughter's future, and the lack of a husband, and therefore she is forced to come to terms with the harsh realities of the present, struggling to make ends meet by selling magazine subscriptions. Edgardo De La Cruz aptly says that Amanda "balances on two worlds—the delusion of memory and the harsh reality of her existence—and she watches with injured desperation both of them crumble before her eyes" (246). She resolves to help her daughter by trying to make her reject her unreal dreamy world of glass animals and face the real world and try to earn a living. As Laura fails to learn typing and drops out of the Rubicam's Business School after a breakdown, Amanda decides on a solution—marriage. On the surface, marriage as a solution seems naive and romantic; it is, however, a very practical and pragmatic decision on Amanda's part. This decision manifests how Amanda is torn between her romantic delusions and her understanding of the harsh realities. As she tells her daughter:

> *AMANDA:* … I know so well what becomes of unmarried women who aren't prepared to occupy a position. I've seen such pitiful cases in the South—barely tolerated spinsters living upon the grudging patronage of sister's husband or brother's wife!—stuck away in some little mousetrap of a room—encouraged by one in-law to visit another—little birdlike women without any nest—eating the crust of humility all their life!
>
> (16)

Marriage, she thinks, will provide her with security, if not love, and she compromises with what she ideally wants. Tom is almost coerced to provide the solution by bringing home a gentleman caller. This almost forced calling of the gentleman caller to dinner and the artificially set-up tête-à-tête and courtship between Laura and Jim O'Connor eventually lead to Jim admitting that he is already engaged; this drives Laura back to the glass menagerie, and, as Bluefarb says, this "is the final touch of pathos that drives Tom Wingfield out of the St. Louis tenement he shares so uncomfortably with mother and sister, out into the world of vagabondage, toward the romance of the sea and the ships, to the presumably freer life of the seafarer" (515). In Scene 4, Amanda praises Tom and Laura, deluding herself, as she always does, saying, "Both of my children—they're *unusual* children! Don't you think I know it? I'm so—*proud!* Happy and—feel I've—so much to be thankful for…" (31). In Scene 6, however, just before Tom enters with Jim, she pathetically exclaims, "Why can't you and your brother be normal people? Fantastic whims and behavior!" (57). As Jim, expected to be a saviour, disappears, all illusions are destroyed, and they are left facing reality. Amanda's silliness vanishes, and she gains what the playwright calls "*dignity and tragic beauty*" (96).

Tom Wingfield

The audience sees the entire action of *The Glass Menagerie* filtered through the consciousness of Tom, the narrator, who says right at the beginning, "The play is memory. Being a memory play, it is dimly lighted, it is sentimental, it is not realistic" (5). Tom's direct address to the audience establishes the fact that the entire play is memory; and it is from this point that the real action begins. Images of entrapment abound in *Menagerie*, and the protagonist manifests a desire for freedom right from the beginning, right from the time the memory begins to unfold. An apparent symbol is the fire escape, the exit from the Wingfield apartment. As Williams himself says, it has "*a touch of accidental poetic truth*" (3) because the huge buildings keep on "*burning with the slow and implacable fires of human desperation*" (3). And it is through the fire escape that Tom frees himself from the domestic world which is suffocating him. Another reason why Tom wishes to escape is because he and Laura are victims of their mother's domination. Tom Donnelly, a New York drama critic who reviewed the play in 1956, referred to Amanda as

> the sensitive human being who in one moment delights in the simple splendors of nature and in another moment is the trapped creature, compulsively poisoning the lives of her children by the very frenzy of her desire to save them, ridiculous in her pretensions but dignified in her refusal to surrender to despair.
>
> (quoted in Dela Cruz 246)

Instead of indulging in his mother's romantic entrapment in the past, Tom, determined not to let her ruin his life completely, seeks adventure and freedom from his family. For Tom, the home becomes a trap from which he must escape to achieve a sense of selfhood and a masculine identity.

Tom emerges as a character no less complex than his mother. Psychoanalysis, says Chodorow, provides an analysis and critique of the reproduction of sex and gender. She says:

> Freud and his followers demonstrated how sexual repression in the family produces the potentially bisexual, polymorphous perverse infant as genitally heterosexual, monogamous adult, with boys appropriating their masculine prerogatives and girls acquiescing in their feminine subordination and passivity. They also demonstrated how closely psychic pain and disorganization (neurosis) were related to these 'normal' outcomes. … The dynamics these accounts describe all result from a male-dominant but father-absent family where women mother.
>
> (40)

After all, the Wingfield household is a male-dominant but a father-absent family; though Tom and Laura's father abandoned the family years back, his "larger-than-life-size photograph" (5) looms large over the Wingfield family, occupying much of their conversation. Chodorow further mentions that

> A boy must attempt to develop a masculine gender identification and learn the masculine role in the absence of a continuous and ongoing personal relationship to his father (and in the absence of a continuously available masculine role model). This positional identification occurs both psychologically and sociologically. … Sociologically, boys

> in father-absent and normally father-remote families develop a sense of what it is to be masculine through identification with cultural images of masculinity and men chosen as masculine models.
>
> (176)

Tom identifies himself with his father and tells Jim O'Connor, "I'm like my father. The bastard son of a bastard!" (62), though his father has been long absent, having abandoned his wife and children many years ago and having fallen in love with long distances instead. Chodorow says that children "whose mothers are available all day but are not responsive or sociable with them may become more 'attached' to their fathers, who are not frequently available but interact intensively and strongly with these infants when they are around" (72). Drawing on a psychoanalytic model of development, Juliet Mitchell, in *Psychoanalysis and Feminism*, points at the early mother–infant relationship and also at the sociological dynamics of an asymmetry in the relationship, stating that, "though socially constructed, [it] is experienced by the child as presocial, or nonsocial. It is the person who intervenes in this relationship—the father—who represents culture and society to the child" (Chodorow 81). Women come to represent the non-social, or the confusion of biological and social, says Chodorow, and men come to "unambiguously represent society" (81). Mr. Wingfield's larger-than-life photograph remains conspicuous, and Tom idolises the masculinity of his absent father. In patriarchal society, says Chodorow, "[b]oys are taught to be masculine more consciously than girls are taught to be feminine" (176). In the absence of her husband, Amanda expects her son to take up the patriarchal 'masculine' roles of provider and protector. Tom seethes within as he is trapped in the artificial world of the shoe factory with its "*celotex interior!*" and its "*—fluorescent—tubes!*" (23). And for various reasons, he thinks of himself as a failure, in social and economic terms, in the masculine roles he needs to play. His job at the warehouse with sixty-five dollars per week is not enough to fulfil the needs of the middle-class household; and because of his love for poetry, a seemingly 'feminine' trait in patriarchal terms, he fails to enjoy camaraderie with his male colleagues, who eye him with scepticism, apathy, or derision. Though he keeps calling himself a poet, Tom constantly tries to free himself from his mother's 'female' influence at home and the dehumanising world of the warehouse.

Unlike his mother Amanda, Tom has had no idyllic past, no world of nostalgia to return to; thus, he cannot escape through yearning. He probably yearns for his absent father, ebullient and romantic, and so he keeps on escaping by indulging in fantasy, in the world of adventure that the movies offer: "Adventure is something I don't have much of at work, so I go to the movies" (33). It remains unclear, however, as to where he goes every night, and when his mother questions him, Tom replies assertively, "Man is by instinct a lover, a hunter, a fighter" (34). In patriarchal cultures, masculine identification is predominantly a gender role identification, in stark contrast to feminine identification, which is predominantly *parental*. D. B. Lynn states, "Males tend to identify with a cultural stereotype of the masculine role; whereas females tend to identify with aspects of their own mother's role specifically" (quoted in Chodorow 176). For a boy/man, the identification processes need not be embedded in and mediated by a real affective relation to his father. In this process of identification:

> he tends to deny identification with and relationship to his mother and reject what he takes to be the feminine world; masculinity is defined as much negatively as positively. Masculine identification processes stress differentiation from others, the denial of affective relation, and categorical universalistic components of the masculine role. Feminine identification processes are relational, whereas masculine identification processes tend to deny relationship.
>
> (Chodorow 176)

In spite of all that Amanda does for her children and in spite of her overprotective concern, Tom identifies with his father and chooses to turn away from his well-meaning mother. Enraged because of his mother's inquisitiveness, he fabricates an odd story, saying, "I'm leading a double-life, a simple honest warehouse worker by day, by night a dynamic *czar* of the *underworld, Mother*" (24). Contrary to his mother's wishes, instead of identifying himself as the ideal son and brother and a father figure to his sister, to fill up the vacuum that has been created by the absent father, he imaginatively identifies himself as a gangster, which connects him to the romantic world of fugitives and outlaws shown in the American movies. Rosefeldt writes,

> [t]he restless sons of absent fathers often see themselves as rebellious outlaws or compulsive petty criminals trying to beat the system (93). Not only does he begin to lie to his mother, he expresses his fascination for Malvolio the stage magician with a miraculous ability to escape from the coffin without removing one nail. These are clear indications that he wishes to free himself from their coffin-like apartment. Tom muses whether it is really possible to escape from a coffin without removing a nail, and [*As if in answer, the father's grinning photo lights up…*]
>
> (28)

Tom's indulgence in these fantasies reminds Amanda of the absent father. Alarmed, she tells him, "You live in a dream; you manufacture illusions" (95).

Tom, who identifies himself with his father, decides to follow in his path. As Paul Rosefeldt says:

> [l]ost and alienated, the sons of the absent father are confused, perplexed, and unsure of their identity. They feel compelled to bring back the father or to follow in his path. In their turmoil, they seek to recreate the father through doubling him, searching for him, creating surrogate fathers, and/or restructuring the father through a series of fraternal relationships.
>
> (86–87)

Consciously or unconsciously, Tom, like all lost sons, emerges as a double of his father. He begins to drink and staying out late like his father. Amanda laments, "More and more you remind me of your father. He was out all hours without explanation!—Then *left! Good bye!*" (35). Tom's mother puts an additional burden on him by expecting him to become a double not of the real father but of the ideal father who provides for the women in the family. In order to analyse and critique the odd Wingfield family, Lori Leathers Single quotes Irene and Herbert Goldenberg, co-authors of *Family Therapy: An Overview*, who proclaim that in families that generate dysfunctional behaviour, "one or both adults and any of the children may be assigned roles inappropriately or be treated as if they have only a single personality characteristic … instead of a wide range of human feelings and attitudes" (quoted in Single 192). Single, in fact, identifies the 'roles' that each of the family members assumes in the absence of husband and father, Mr. Wingfield Senior. In keeping with the terms used by the Goldenbergs, Single refers to Amanda as the "rejected parent" (quoted 192) type, who seeks gratification through her idealised past and through her children. Laura, physically crippled, frail, and fragile, becomes the "scapegoat" in this case, the "identified-patient who is carrying the pathology for the entire family" and also the "symptom bearer … expressing a family's 'disequilibrium'" (quoted 192). And poor Tom emerges as the "parentified-child" (quoted 192). Amanda constantly coerces her son Tom to take up the responsibilities of the husband and father who abandoned them sixteen years back. She says to her son, "I've had to put up a solitary battle all these years. But you're my right-hand bower! Don't fall down, don't fail!" (30). Yet, knowing fully well that her son is looking for an opportunity to escape, Amanda says that she may grant him permission to leave, "But not till there's somebody to take your place" (35). Instead of shouldering that responsibility as the parentified child, Tom transfers that burden to Jim O'Connor, who seems to be a saviour, the father-double, one that Amanda thinks will indeed be that someone to fill in the vacuum that had been created by Mr. Wingfield's disappearance, the "long delayed but always expected something that we live for" (5). Hopeful about Laura's future, Amanda tries, consciously or unconsciously, to recreate the meeting she had with Mr. Wingfield, the now-absent father. She tells Laura that she is wearing the dress she wore on "the day I met your father" (53), and she brings out her wedding silver to serve Jim. Jim O'Connor, the gentleman caller, seemingly a saviour, appears briefly only to disappear. And Tom disappoints Amanda by not becoming the ideal father figure but by following the path of the romantic father who escaped the burdens of family life. Tom inevitably follows the father who has been "absent going on sixteen years" and is still "grinning" (62); he too seeks a way out of the confines of the home into a world of adventure.

Tom is nicknamed 'Shakespeare' by Jim, who feels that his friend is somewhat strange, not normal, set apart from the others. Though he is called Shakespeare by Jim, Tom is not really a poet. He is not a romantic either. He tells the audience that he was fired from the shoe warehouse for writing poetry on the lid of a shoe box. One may ask, does a poet write on a shoe box? One may also ask, does Tom's running away make him a romantic and a poet? Bluefarb rightly points out, "[f]or his poetry writing and his seafaring are not so much the gestures of a young man searching for the *ultima Thule* of romance, as they are the expression of a man's desperation to escape the drab present and a past that prevents that present from fulfilling itself in a future" (515–516). Instead of being an act of an oblivious poet, writing poetry on a shoe box could be an excuse, or the conscious act of rebellion, so that he gets fired from the warehouse. He lacks the poet's sensitivity or the sympathy to handle the eccentricities of the romantic delusional mother trapped in her past. Thus, coupled with this rebellious act in the warehouse comes rebellion against his domineering yet romantic mother. His escape is not the quick impulsive act of the romantic poet but one deliberately planned; he keeps on enquiring at the seamen's union hall and buys his union card surreptitiously using the household funds. Manifesting neither empathy nor sympathy, Tom decides not to indulge at all in Amanda's romantic delusions and resolves to leave his mother and his sister. He finally exercises his freedom and proves his manhood by abandoning them. Tom's decision to turn away and separate himself from his mother and sister initially seems akin to the irresponsible abandonment by his father. The situation that almost forces him to abandon them is indeed pathetic. Amanda coerces Tom to bring home a gentleman caller for Laura, and Tom invites Jim to dinner. The Wingfield family spends a lot of money decorating their apartment, Laura sheds her shyness and fear in the presence of the warm and sympathetic Jim, and yet finally comes the revelation that Jim is already engaged, a fact Tom was unaware of. Laura returns to the brittle world of her glass animals, the menagerie, and Tom runs away to being a vagabond and drifter instead of indulging any more in the artificial escapes he has had in the movie houses. Interestingly, as Chodorow says, "Turning from mother (and father) represents independence and individuation, progress, activity, and participation in the real world" (82). Indeed, in the West, boys acquire manhood and define their masculine identity by separating themselves from the mother. In Tom's case, this running away ironically makes him a man in traditional patriarchal terms. As Joan Riviere says, "It is by turning away from our mother that we finally become, by our different paths, grown men and women" (quoted in Chodorow 82).

Tom joins the Merchant Marine, an all-male setting, and his decision may be viewed as his conscious effort to eschew the feminine associations and be part of a masculine social space. In her study titled *Between Men*, Eve Sedgewick claims that men, seeking to escape the feminine, enter a 'homosocial' realm, "neither heterosexual nor homosexual, but outside of the domestic, away from the feminine where men find 'non-threatening community in the company of other men'" (quoted in Kidd 47). Millie M. Kidd brings the reader's attention to the epigraph to Williams's *The Glass Menagerie*, which is the last line of the E. E. Cummings poem "somewhere I have never travelled, gladly beyond," stating that critics have used the poem to interpret the play in myriad ways. The last line of the poem says, "nobody, not even the rain, has such small hands." She says that many of those critics who address Williams's use of the poem "associate its imagery—frailty, enclosure, open/closed, Spring, rose, flower, death, eyes, hands, and rain—with Laura" (47). In traditional patriarchal society, these qualities are generally associated with the feminine. Many critics also believe that Tom, perceiving these feminine qualities as a trap, wishes to escape. Continuing the same line of argument based on the findings of Chodorow, one can state that Tom must escape from this entrapment in order to achieve selfhood and to acquire a masculine identity. But Kidd argues that the poem's imagery deconstructs this idea: "the speaker of the poem sees the feminine not as a threat or a trap but rather as a necessary part of a masculine identity that is more fluid and multiple than the imposed cultural model" (47). Even if one views Tom's flight as a flight towards independence, one needs to remember that as he disentangles himself from the domestic ties and the feminine, he simultaneously fails to conform to the rugged masculine culture he has run to. Like Cummings, Williams challenged rigid social codes of behaviour all his life, and Tom manifests the tension experienced, as the playwright himself did, measuring himself against the social construct of maleness. Coerced by his mother but finding it impossible to conform to the cultural model of masculinity, Tom attempts to reject the feminine forces in his life and find his male identity in an idealised masculine setting by deciding to join the Merchant Marine, but he finds himself on the margins of society, haunted by Laura, who embodies the feminine in himself. The Williams siblings, with only sixteen months between them, were inseparable as twins and were often called 'The Couple.' Kidd too asserts that Williams had Laura as well as Rose in mind when he selected the epigraph, adding that the presence of the Cummings poem also throws light on the playwright's own struggle to achieve a balance between the masculine and the feminine. He says:

> Much of Cummings' poetry undermines the social models of masculine and feminine and offers instead a more fluid sexual identity, one that goes beyond gender boundaries of 'you' and 'me' or 'he' and 'she' to a genderless 'us,' a territory with no fixed gender roles. This blurring of boundaries occurs in the second stanza … where the flower, later referred to specifically as a rose, is both the beloved and the lover who is also the speaker of the poem.
>
> (49)

The rose may be associated with Rose/Laura; after all, Jim's nickname for her was 'Blue Roses,' and it may also be associated with Tennessee Williams/ Tom Wingfield. Viewed in this light, Laura and those feminine qualities that she embodies may be viewed as positive feminine influences on Tom, influences that 'open' him or lead him to other possibilities. The possibilities include the feminine in Nature and in Tom's own nature. Tom fails to leave behind this feminine part of himself. In another poem, Cummings wrote, "one's not half two. It's two are halves of one." The feminine half is the one half that Tom fails to leave behind. An issue which did not really bother audiences when *The Glass Menagerie* was staged might be worthy of mention here. The question as to where Tom goes every night remains unanswered. He repeatedly says that he goes to the movies, but that does not sound very convincing, and his mother reacts sharply.

> *AMANDA:* I think you've been doing things that you're ashamed of. That's why you act like this. I don't believe that you go every night to the movies. Nobody goes to the movies night after night. Nobody in their right mind goes to the movies as often as you pretend to. People don't go to the movies at nearly midnight, and movies don't let out at two A.M. Come in stumbling. Muttering to yourself like a maniac!
>
> (23)

Bottoms and various other critics have suggested that the issue could be controversial, that Tom, like the playwright himself, could be gay. Bottoms says that *The Glass Menagerie* can be seen as an example of a 'closet drama' in which homosexuality is never mentioned "but into which those 'in the know' can read a hidden gay subtext" (lxxix). But it could also be said that *The Glass Menagerie* reflects Williams's struggle to represent a sexual identity that is neither masculine nor feminine but fluid. As Kidd says, keeping Cummings in mind, each individual who is part of a couple retains his/her uniqueness, and though part of a unity, the individuals are composed of many elements, and that includes both masculine and feminine attributes. A failure he may be, in traditional, social, patriarchal terms, yet Tom succeeds in evading the rigid categories of gender.

The final question remains whether Tom finds what he seeks—freedom. Though it seems that Tom has had a romantic escape, he remains "tied, through guilt, to his own immediate past" (Bluefarb 515). This is how the play ends:

> *TOM:* ... Blow out your candles, Laura—and so good-bye....
> [*She blows the candles out.*]
>
> (97)

Having plunged into an uncertain future and preferring that to a bleak deadening present, worsened by Amanda's constant nagging and interference, Tom, one understands, has rushed headlong into a world which is harsher. Tom never really succeeds in running away from his past. He reawakens the past with the image of his sister, whom he has lost. As his memory ends, as the narrator in the present, he ironically reveals himself a drifter without direction and without identity.

Laura Wingfield

It would be interesting to note that the origins of the play *The Glass Menagerie* lie in a short story titled "Portrait of a Girl in Glass" that Williams wrote in 1941. It all began with a series of plays, which were to be called the "Mississippi Sketches," and this included a comedy with the title, "The Front Porch Girl." This portrayed a shy girl, similar to Laura, who finds a companion in one of the lodgers of her mother's boarding house. This was expanded into a play called *If You Breathe, it Breaks!* And then it became the short story titled, "Portrait of a Girl in Glass." The plot of *If You Breathe, it Breaks!* is centred on a lady named Mrs. Wingfield and her children, a girl and two boys. The girl manifests a love for her glass menagerie, and the mother, concerned about her daughter, wishes that her daughter would be introduced to a gentleman caller. Both the play and the short story featured the daughter who sat in the front porch of her house, awaiting gentlemen callers, and also found consolation in a menagerie of glass animals which, as C.W.E. Bigsby says, "becomes an expression of the fragility she believes characterizes those so easily broken by the world" (37). Soon Williams signed a contract with Metro-Goldwyn-Mayer and wrote a script for Hollywood titled *The Gentleman Caller*, which featured a woman awaiting a gentleman caller. And, finally, Williams revised it and shaped it into *The Glass Menagerie*.

One of the two principal metaphors or symbols in *The Glass Menagerie* is obviously glass, and glass features in the title itself. Laura, the painfully shy girl in *The Glass Menagerie*, is constantly associated with glass. Indeed, hers is also a portrait of a girl in glass. Williams refers to "the lovely fragility of glass which is her image." Associated with the brittle translucency of glass, Laura is imbued with a "pristine clarity such as light used in early religious portraits of female saints or madonnas." Bigsby reminds us that the final play version differs from the short story; the story lacked "that detailed social and political context which broadened the metaphoric significance of *The Glass Menagerie*" (36). In the play, Laura is given a deformed foot; in the story, the flaw is worse. As Bigsby writes, "She is mentally rather than physically fragile" (36). The girl in the story believes, at the age of twenty, that stars are five-pointed because they are represented likewise on the Star of Bethlehem which she fixes on top of her Christmas tree. She thinks of the characters in her favourite book as real. The story too has a gentleman caller, though not from the same high school as in the play. She responds to him because he resembles a character from her book. Interestingly, there is an echo of that in *Menagerie* when Laura addresses Jim as Freckles, the protagonist of the novel titled *Freckles*, which is not alluded to in the play.

Though not as mentally unstable as the girl in "Portrait of a Girl in Glass," Laura manifests a social ineptitude; she lacks the social intelligence to understand the need for preparing herself to earn a living.

> *AMANDA:* I went to the typing instructor and introduced myself as your mother. She didn't know who you were. "Wingfield," she said. "We don't have any such student enrolled at the school!"
>
> ...
>
> "I wonder," she said, "If you could be talking about that terribly shy little girl who dropped out of school after only a few days' attendance?"
>
> ...
>
> And she said, "No—I remember her perfectly now. Her hands shook so that she couldn't hit the right keys! The first time we gave a speed-test, she broke down completely—was sick at the stomach and almost had to be carried into the wash room! After that morning she never showed up any more. We phoned the house but never got any answer" ...
>
> (13–14)

Coerced by Amanda, she joins the Rubicam's Business School to learn typing and shorthand but eventually drops out after a nervous breakdown. This is how the conversation runs:

> *AMANDA:* Laura, where have you been going when you've gone out pretending that you were going to business college ?
>
> *LAURA:* I've just been going out walking.
>
> …
>
> *AMANDA:* Walking? Walking? In winter? Deliberately courting pneumonia in that light coat? Where did you walk to, Laura?
>
> *LAURA:* All sorts of places—mostly in the park.
>
> …
>
> [*Screen image: Winter scene in a park.*]
>
> I couldn't go back there. I—threw up—on the floor!
>
> *AMANDA:* From half past seven till after five every day you mean to tell me you walked around in the park, because you wanted to make me think that you were still going to Rubicam's Business College?
>
> *LAURA:* It wasn't as bad as it sounds. I went inside places to get warmed up.
>
> *AMANDA:* Inside where?
>
> *LAURA:* I went in the art museum and the bird-houses at the Zoo. I visited the penguins every day! Sometimes I did without lunch and went to the movies. Lately I've been spending most of my afternoons in the Jewel-Box, that big glass-house where they raise the tropical flowers.
>
> (14–15)

Laura keeps on pretending to attend the secretarial course at the business school, but in her aimless meanderings, she somewhat resembles her brother—walking around in the park, going to the movies, going to the art museum, and visiting penguins at the zoo every day. As she is confronted by her indignant mother, who demands to know why she hid everything from her, one finds that there are two kinds of fears working within her: she once again feels terrified with the memory of the course, and she is also terrified of the disappointment she has caused her mother. Her social ineptitude makes her take refuge in her glass collection, the eponymous glass menagerie, and her father's old phonograph records. The rose symbolism underscores Laura's strangeness and abnormality. As Single mentions, the screen image of blue roses symbolises Laura's peculiarity, adding that just as red is a hot colour, blue is a cold one. She says, "If red roses are the traditional symbol of romantic love, then blue roses must symbolize Laura's lack of passion" (198), adding that though blue is the wrong colour to associate with roses, it is the right colour for Laura. Jim O'Connor also feels that Blue Roses is an appropriate nickname for Laura since she is different from everyone else.

Rosefeldt refers to children of absent fathers as "lost children" (23), failures alienated from themselves and the world that surrounds them, who "live in a wasteland, a world of mourning and melancholia, filled with sterile objects, an illusory world that is often crumbling around them" (23). In *Menagerie*, one finds a world of glass figurines and Victrola records, a melancholic world full of sterile objects indeed, a world to which Laura retreats. Rosefeldt's description of 'lost children' befits not just Laura but also Tom, incessantly yearning for affection and steeped in nostalgia. As Tom says about his sister, "She lives in a world of her own—a world of little glass ornaments, Mother…." (48). The menagerie traps Laura with its pristine beauty and austerity. As she finds contentment in the world of her glass animals, she also refrains from seeking happiness from the outside world. Laura knows that she is "crippled" (17), a condition which to her mother, however, is "a little defect—hardly noticeable, even!" (17). Sam Bluefarb points out, "Laura, unlike her brother and her mother, *can* face the present—but only to the extent that she recognizes the truth about herself in that present" (516). She is acutely aware of her physical defect, a lame foot that forces her to wear leg braces. The leg braces sound to her like thunder, and they embarrass her so much that she shies away from human contact. There could be two explanations: it could mean that Laura sees her lameness as a true infirmity, though her mother refuses to do so, or it could mean that she uses her physical debility as an excuse to avoid human contact. As Bluefarb rightly says, "Laura's infirmity has affected and thus determined her attitude toward the world. Her entire personality has been forced to turn in upon itself; driven into the mold of her desperation and, finally, resignation" (516). She surrenders to the unchanging world of her glass animals, wishing to escape from the mundane everyday world and the world of the present into a world of fantasy and delusion bereft of her lameness—a defect she is painfully aware of, no matter how much her mother tries to hide it with euphemisms.

It is entirely Amanda's decision to get Laura a husband so that she can evade being like other spinsters, "little birdlike women without any nest" (16), and she is coerced to accept her gentleman caller Jim O'Connor, her brother's co-worker. In fact, in the absence of the real patriarch, the father, another patriarch, her brother Tom, takes charge of things in a bid to secure her future. As Kaja Silverman has observed in *The Subject of Semiotics*, many cinematic narratives are "organized around a demonstration and an interrogation of the female's castrated condition" (quoted in Crandell 7). The patriarchal gaze that falls upon the female protagonist is employed as a signifier of castration or lack – Silverman mentions the lack "of control, power, privilege" (quoted in Crandell 7). As Tom directs his gaze upon the women of the household, he underscores their most important lack, the lack of a husband. And then Tom directs his gaze and attention to the exquisitely fragile Laura with other inadequacies too. Most of Tom's conversations are centred on Laura's lacks and shortcomings, traits like her fragility, her crippled state, and her unpopularity owing to her shyness—traits her mother denies—and also her lack of a husband. To fill up these inadequacies, Tom agrees to side with his mother and decides to 'arrange' for a gentleman caller for Laura.

In contrast to the man's active role, the woman's role is usually that of the passive recipient of the male gaze. Amanda, in spite of her domineering nature, accepts the male gaze. On the night the gentleman caller is supposed to visit, the object of attention is her daughter, but it is she who gleefully announces, "I'm going to make a spectacular appearance!" (53). It is from this point that Laura's actions begin to show traits of an amount of strength. Laura desists from her mother's efforts to make her look (sexually) attractive. Amanda stuffs Laura's bosom with powder puffs wrapped in handkerchiefs, but Laura removes them. Studying relations between men and women, John Berger notes, in *Ways of Seeing* that "Men look at women. Women watch themselves being looked at" (quoted in Crandell 8). This is precisely what Amanda wants, that Laura may learn to enjoy being looked at. She thinks that once Laura is made conscious of her good looks, the consciousness itself will lead Laura to try to attract the gentleman caller and eventually also secure a husband. As Crandell mentions, Laura "actively resists both the role that society prescribes for women as well as Amanda's insistence that she conform to it" (9). Amanda reprimands her daughter thus: "You couldn't be satisfied with just sitting home, and yet whenever I try to arrange something for you, you seem to resist it" (52). Laura refuses to open the door when the gentleman caller arrives with her brother. And she refuses to be seen, actively resisting the male gaze. As the gentleman caller enters the apartment, it becomes impossible for Laura to avoid him, yet she tries to evade his gaze. For one brief moment, she succeeds. Jim enters the dining room and places the lighted candelabrum on the floor, and Laura intentionally takes a seat on the opposite side, prompting Jim to say, "I can't hardly see you sitting way over there" (72). Interestingly, Laura's 'female gaze' is upon Jim, and she says, "I can—see you" (72). Jim resists the female gaze, stating "that's not fair, I'm in the limelight" (72), and after this brief reversal of patriarchal roles, Laura lets herself be seen, moving in in the orbit of light. Jim manifests delight and satisfaction as he says, "Good! Now I can see you!" (72). Crandell rightly says, "[a]s much as Jim wants to see, Laura prefers to remain invisible, but given that impossibility, she becomes like a transparent piece of glass, both resisting and succumbing to Jim's penetrating gaze" (9). In stark contrast to her mother, Laura emerges as a woman who resists the male gaze in *The Glass Menagerie* and comes to represent an alternative to those complying with the conventional role of women in a patriarchal society.

The coming of Jim O'Connor as Laura's only gentleman caller holds a special significance. Earlier in the play, her memory of Jim, her one and only infatuation in high school, has already been revealed, a memory much cherished. It is a memory that involves an amusing nickname that he had for her—Blue Roses. She has revealed that she remembers sitting through three of his performances in an opera in the hope of getting his autograph. Laura has also remembered his engagement to another girl. So far, Jim had remained an illusion for Laura, but as he visits her as the gentleman caller and a possible suitor, the cherished memory shows the potential of turning to reality.

As Tom announces the imminent visit of the gentleman caller, he also urges his mother not to expect too much. Amanda, paying no heed to her son, asks Laura to make a wish on the moon, "A little silver slipper of a moon" (49). The image of the moon is congenial to romance, but the slipper image brings up an expectation of the fulfilment of the Cinderella story. The slipper image also anticipates the later dancing between Laura and Jim, her Prince Charming. But Jim, after all, is no Prince Charming, the slipper does not fit the 'crippled' Princess, and the illusion is destroyed. But much happens before that. Glenn Man calls the dramatisation of Laura's dream world "a classic achievement of the modern stage" (25). Laura is drawn out of her cocoon slowly by the warm and charming Jim O'Connor, whose eagerness and encouragement make her talk without restraint, a trait hitherto unseen by the audience. Though she continues to be reticent, speaking in very short sentences, she talks about his singing in high school, their past affinities, her leg brace and the self-consciousness and embarrassment associated with it, Jim's old girlfriend, and more. She brings out her copy of their high school yearbook, and after all these years, Laura receives the long-coveted autograph on the opera sheet and also learns that Jim had broken off the engagement she had come to know about long back. Williams mentions in a stage direction how she is experiencing "*the climax of her secret life*" (70). But contrary to what her mother wanted, Jim's encouragement exposes her vulnerability too like never before, and she is eventually shattered one more time.

Before Jim and Laura begin to dance, she shows him her glass menagerie, including the unicorn, which is a horse unlike the other horses because of its horn. Frank Durham says that generally the glass menagerie, including the unicorn, "portrays Laura, her fragility, her delicacy, her beauty, her unworldliness" (66). Indeed, Laura is rare, as Jim says, "Shy, huh? It's unusual to meet a shy girl nowadays" (58), and her brother also says such "terribly shy" (58) girls are indeed extinct. One of Williams's stage directions connects her to glass yet one more time: "[*she is like a piece of translucent glass touched by light, given a momentary radiance, not actual, not lasting*]" (51). Through the dance, Jim enters Laura's dream world, but he is ironically instrumental in breaking the brittle, fragile glass-like Laura just as he breaks the unicorn, both by accident. The breaking of the horn of the unicorn could be looked upon as a parallel of Rose's lobotomy. As Laura says, she would imagine that her unicorn has "had an operation. The horn was removed to make him feel less—freakish" (86). That her world of dreams has had the risk of being shattered has been shown quite early in the play. After a terrible row, Tom, having called Amanda a witch, in sheer anger, hurls his coat across the room, striking Laura's glass collection and shattering some of them, leaving her distraught by the inadvertent damage. In stark contrast, here she responds to the breaking of the horn of the unicorn differently. Calling it "a blessing in disguise" (86), she shows tremendous strength as she says, "It's no tragedy Freckles. Glass breaks so easily. No matter how careful you are. The traffic jars the shelves and things fall off them" (86). Her words are moving and expressive, and as Thomas F. Van Laan points out, "[t]his is not the voice of a shy girl withdrawn from reality and obsessed with a grossly inferior substitute for genuine experience. It is, rather, the voice of someone wholly at ease with reality and quite capable of accepting the less pleasant facts of life" (249). Laura addresses him by this private nickname, Freckles, and this is the only time it is used or mentioned in the play. The name Freckles actually came from the short story "Portrait of a Girl in Glass," where the girl is shown to be fascinated with the eponymous romantic hero in the novel titled *Freckles*.

Laura's sweet dignity and becoming stoicism after being let down by her first and only gentleman caller make Gassner say, "she is an unforgettable bit of Marie Laurencin painting" (392). Jim has not viewed Laura as a 'cripple' and has enjoyed her company, and as he kisses her, it seems that her long-cherished dream has at last become real. But, unfortunately, as she is relishing the moments, she fails to realise that Jim has evoked yet another illusion in her, the illusion of their being partners for life. Laura's reawakened hopes are crushed. The shattering of her self is manifested in her behavioural change, and her speech breaks down. In stark contrast to her conversations so far, candid and without restraint, she responds to Jim's utterances only with a short fragmented sentence: "You —won't—call again?" (89) as Jim tells her that he has been "going steady … with a girl named Betty" (89). Ironically, Jim goes on talking about his fiancée, Betty, adding that the "power of love is really pretty tremendous! Love is something that—changes the whole world, Laura!" (90). After his effusive statements, Jim, however, becomes painfully conscious that Laura has stopped conversing. Somewhat embarrassed, he says, "I wish that you would—say something" (90). Instead of saying anything, she just gives him the broken unicorn. Jim wants to know the verbal interpretation of this symbol, and she manages to say that it is a souvenir. From this moment to the one in which Jim leaves, Laura speaks only one more word, "Yes" (94), that too prompted by her mother. As Van Laan says, "[u]tterly devastated by her one attempt to thrive in the real world, Laura has been thrust back into a secret life that no longer exists" (249). Amanda encourages Laura to wish Jim O'Connor "luck—and happiness—and success!" (94), and after Jim leaves, the audience finds her crouching "*beside the Victrola to wind it*" (94). She knows that she must again escape to her father's old phonograph records and her little glass animals. Though crestfallen herself, Amanda tries to comfort Laura, who responds with a smile, a smile without hope or promise.

Jim O'Connor: The Gentleman Caller

Worried about her daughter, who does not have any work to sustain herself, Amanda decides that marriage will be an easier solution because her husband would provide for her. She has to concede that, unlike her, Laura will not be lucky enough to be wooed by a scion of an aristocratic family from the South, and Amanda will have to accept, as a possible suitor for Laura, an ordinary man. Amanda indeed accepts someone that Tom recommends, a co-worker from the shoe warehouse, Jim O'Connor. It so happens that this Jim O'Connor is the same person Laura secretly loved and worshipped during her high school days, the same boy who used to call Laura Blue Roses. Both siblings remember him as the high school hero—senior class president, star basketball player, and member of the debating society—the cynosure of all eyes, a hero always in the limelight. The second act, in fact, begins with a soliloquy which, Thomas L. King says, like the first, "strikes something of a balance between irony and nostalgia" (213). Tom's first description of Jim is indeed laden with nostalgia; his discourse indicates that, like his sister, he too was awed by Jim. Tom says:

> In high school, Jim was a hero. He had tremendous Irish good nature and vitality with the scrubbed and polished look of white chinaware. He seemed to move in a continual spotlight. He was a star in basketball, captain of the debating club, president of the senior class and the glee club, and he sang the male lead in the annual light operas. He was always running or bounding, never just walking. He seemed always at the point of defeating the law of gravity.
>
> (50)

In spite of the tremendous hero worship and awe, Tom soon introduces mild mockery in his diction, which soon turns to a stronger sneer. He says:

> He was shooting with such velocity through his adolescence that you would logically expect him to arrive at nothing short of the White House by the time he was thirty. But Jim apparently ran into more interference after his graduation from Soldan. His speed had definitely slowed. Six years after he left high school he was holding a job that wasn't much better than mine.
>
> (50)

The audience/reader is made to understand that after his graduation, the young gentleman has failed to fulfil the promise of his high school years. The young gentleman who showed so much potential has turned out to be no better than Tom, working as a clerk in a shoe warehouse. Jim is really not to be blamed, however, for working in the warehouse, and nor is Tom. As mentioned in Chapter 1, between 1929 and 1932, wages declined by 60 percent, and the national income fell from $81 billion to $41 billion.

Jim speaks of his plans of enrolling in a night school course where he would take up radio engineering and public speaking, and he epitomises the American dream of success, glorified in the romances of Horatio Alger. This ambition is what endears Jim to Amanda, the ambition which, she thinks, will eventually compensate for the lack of glory and success in the post-high school years. Jim shows the promise of being the mythical American 'self-made man.' Heike Paul says that, historically, the notion has been established that upward mobility in American society, in sharp contrast to European societies, is illimitable no matter what one's inherited social and financial status. He mentions European visitors to America in the 19th century—Alexis de Tocqueville, Joanna Trollope, Harriet Martineau, and James Bryce—who have remarked "on the hectic commercial activities of Americans and considered their peculiar pursuit of material gain as an aspect of the American national character" (367–368). Theodor W. Adorno, who visited America in the 20th century, also identified a culturally specific "barbarian success religion" (quoted in Paul 368) in American society. Paul adds that, in its hegemonic version, the myth of the self-made man refers to "expressive individualism and individual success … connected to utopian visions of a classless society, or at least to a society that allows considerable social mobility" (368). With education, hard work, and discipline, the self-made man aimed "at the sheer accumulation of property, recognition, prestige, and personal gain" (370). The author of pop fiction, Alger canonised this myth of the self-made man. He had a steady stream of 'rags-to-riches' stories, about a hundred novels, each with similar plots, which showed how a poor and virtuous boy rose to middle-class respectability by honesty, perseverance, and hard work. By sheer luck, Alger's typical protagonist has a chance encounter with benevolent and useful friends, or a chance encounter with a gentleman who becomes his mentor, and thus the reward for his good deeds and success is almost always precipitated by a stroke of good luck.

Earlier in the play, Amanda is shown to be a firm believer in the American dream of success and her trust in the myth of the self-made man. "Try and you will *succeed*!" (31), she tells her son when he shows dissatisfaction with his work in the shoe factory; her response is the traditional motto of the American dream of success. In *The Glass Menagerie*, however, it is not Amanda but Jim, arriving as an "emissary from a world of reality" (5), who may be called the chief spokesman for the American dream. To Jim, the warehouse, instead of being a prison, as it is to Tom, becomes a rung in the ladder towards future success. He believes that his future triumph lies in self-improvement through education, in this case a night course. As he says:

> Because I believe in the future of television! [*turning his back to her*.] I wish to be ready to go right up along with it. Therefore I'm planning to get in on the ground floor. In fact I've already made the right connections and all that remains is for the industry itself to get under way! Full steam!—[*His eyes are starry*.] *Knowledge*—Zzzzzp! *Money*—Zzzzzzp!— *Power*! That's the cycle democracy is built on!
>
> (82)

This is followed by a Dale Carnegie–style lecture on self-confidence. Self-help books connected individuals to the ideology of self-making and to the myth of the self-made man. A fine example of such a book would be Carnegie's *How to Win Friends and Influence People* (1936). The book had seventeen print editions in its first year of publishing and sold 2,50,000 copies in the first three months. As Steven Watts says, Carnegie has been applauded for having created a new and attractive blend of "success ideology, charismatic personality and self-fulfilment, positive thought, human relations, and therapeutic well-being" (7). In spite of Jim's confident discourse, there emerges a contradiction. With an apt reference to Malcolm Cowley, Robert L. McDonald points out that in Depression-era America, there was "a pervasive de-emphasis of individuality in favor of concern for the 'group' … the thirties were a time when virtually everyone was swept along in 'a daydream of revolutionary brotherhood,' living a collective passion" (60). In terms of sociology, then, American society was moving in an opposite direction as Jim continued with his efforts of mastering the essentials of public speaking to smoothen his individualistic climb up the ladder of capitalism. This issue is summed up beautifully by Hieke Paul:

> Success stories thus can easily be considered American fairy tales with a providential twist, and as such they echo in and are invoked by many cultural productions from 19th century popular fiction to 20th- and 21st-century Hollywood films. Their protagonist, the self-made man, personifies the American dream as wishful thinking and wish-fulfillment at the same time … As part dream, part fantasy, and part prophecy, the foundational myth of the self-made man seems to be powerful enough to defy the overwhelming evidence of its own baselessness.
>
> (379)

All of this gives rise to an apprehension that, just like the Wingfields, the gentleman caller Jim is also harbouring illusions. He has failed to live up to the promise he showed in high school, and he will probably fail to achieve success in spite of his night school training.

Jim's ordinariness is shown in the play through the unicorn/horse symbolism. The symbolism of the glass menagerie, including the unicorn, is usually associated with the beauty and fragility of Laura. Frank Durham feels that the unicorn symbolises the illusion Laura sustained all her life—her idealised concept of Jim, the 'hero'. The audience meets a Jim of whom Tom speaks with a bit of sarcasm and bitterness, an ordinary and frustrated human being who, however, likes and values Tom as he was "someone who could remember his former glory, who had seen him win basketball games and the silver cup in debating" (50). Laura, still retaining her illusions and still awestruck, entrusts the unicorn in his hands, also warning him, "Oh, be careful—if you breathe, it breaks!" (83). With the full knowledge that unicorns are special because they are "extinct in the modern world" (83), he knocks the unicorn from the table during the dance with Laura and breaks its horn—something that had made the unicorn different from the other horses. It could be said that Jim, as distinct and special as the unicorn with the horn, sinks into being someone ordinary, "himself destroying the aura of distinctiveness which Laura gave him, destroying her illusion" (Durham 10).

It may be said that Jim is posed as a saviour in this Friday night supper. There is an air of expectancy in spite of Tom's request not to expect too much; the mother indulges in a ritualistic dressing of Laura, and the women wait for his arrival. Jim's arrival is marked by the advent of rain, and there are hopes of fertility (marriage) and renewal. Sounds emerge from a dance hall ironically bearing the name Paradise Dance Hall, where couples kiss "behind ashpits and telephone poles" (39). Tom says that it is "the compensation for lives that passed like mine, without any change or adventure" (39), foreboding that Laura's life will not change after all.

After dinner, there is a power-cut, and Amanda jokingly asks, "Where was Moses when the lights went out?" (67). This once again shows her expectation of a Moses-like saviour who would lead his people to a new Canaan, as it were. The answer to her joke, however, is "In the dark" (67). Jim fails in his attempts to play the modern saviour. The cruel joke ironically comes true as Laura and Amanda continue to remain in the dark. As Jim O'Connor, expected to be a saviour, appears only to disappear from the lives of the Wingfields and as their illusions are shattered, there comes a sense of desolation. In the final lines, Tom reveals that infinite gloominess and desolation as he says, "For nowadays the world is lit by lightning! Blow out your candles, Laura—and so goodbye…" (97).

Bibliography

Primary Text

Williams, Tennessee. *The Glass Menagerie*, edited by Stephen J. Bottoms, Methuen Drama India-Bloomsbury, 2015.

References

Bigsby, C.W.E. "Entering the Glass Menagerie." *The Cambridge Companion to Tennessee Williams*, edited by Matthew C. Roudane, Cambridge University Press, 1997, pp. 29–44.

Bluefarb, Sam. "The Glass Menagerie: Three Visions of Time." *College English*, Vol. 24, No. 7, 1963, pp. 513–18. *JSTOR*, https://doi.org/10.2307/372877. Accessed 6 Mar. 2024.

Bottoms, Stephen J. "The Glass Menagerie." *A Student Handbook to the Plays of Tennessee Williams*, edited by Katherine Weiss, Methuen Drama India-Bloomsbury, 2021. pp. 17–82.

Chodorow, Nancy J. *The Reproduction of Mothering: Psychoanalysis and the Sociology of Gender*. University of California Press, 1978.

Crandell, George W. "The Cinematic Eye in Tennessee Williams's *The Glass Menagerie*." *The Tennessee Williams Annual Review*, no. 1, 1998, pp. 1–11. *JSTOR*, https://doi.org/10.2307/45343903. Accessed 6 Mar. 2024.

Dela Cruz, Edgardo. "Things Loved; Things Remembered: Joaquin's 'Portrait' and 'Williams' 'Menagerie'." *Philippine Studies*, Vol. 14, No. 2, 1966, pp. 243–52. *JSTOR*, http://www.jstor.org/stable/42720097. Accessed 6 Mar. 2024.

Durham, Frank. "Tennessee Williams, Theatre Poet in Prose." *South Atlantic Bulletin*, Vol. 36, No. 2, 1971, pp. 3–16. *JSTOR*, https://doi.org/10.2307/3197257. Accessed 6 Mar. 2024.

Fritscher, John J. "SOME ATTITUDES AND A POSTURE: Religious Metaphor and Ritual in Tennessee Williams' Query of the American God." *Modern Drama*, Vol. 13, 1970, pp. 201–215. https://jackfritscher.com/Academic/Tenn_Williams_ModernDrama2.html. Accessed 7 Mar. 2024.

Gassner, John. "Tennessee Williams: Dramatist of Frustration." *The English Journal*, Vol. 37, No. 8, 1948, pp. 387–93. *JSTOR*, https://doi.org/10.2307/807030. Accessed 7 Mar. 2024.

Kidd, Millie M. "E. E. Cummings and *The Glass Menagerie*." *Spring*, no. 11, 2002, pp. 47–51. *JSTOR*, http://www.jstor.org/stable/43915129. Accessed 7 Mar. 2024.

King, Thomas L. "Irony and Distance in *The Glass Menagerie*." *Educational Theatre Journal*, Vol. 25, No. 2, 1973, pp. 207–14. *JSTOR*, https://doi.org/10.2307/3205871. Accessed 7 Mar. 2024.

Man, Glenn. "Memory as Technique and Theme in *The Glass Menagerie* and *The Death of a Salesman*." *Notre Dame English Journal*, Vol. 5, No. 2, 1970, pp. 23–30. *JSTOR*, http://www.jstor.org/stable/40066506. Accessed 8 Mar. 2024.

McDonald, Robert L. "'By Instinct': The Problem of Identity in *The Glass Menagerie*." *CEA Critic*, Vol. 59, No. 3, 1997, pp. 58–64. *JSTOR*, http://www.jstor.org/stable/44377194. Accessed 8 Mar. 2024.

Paul, Heike. "Expressive Individualism and the Myth of the Self-Made Man." *The Myths That Made America: An Introduction to American Studies*, Transcript Verlag, 2014, pp. 367–420. *JSTOR*, http://www.jstor.org/stable/j.ctv1wxsdq.11. Accessed 8 Mar. 2024.

Reid, Desmond. "Tennessee Williams." *Studies: An Irish Quarterly Review*, Vol. 46, No. 184, 1957, pp. 431–46. *JSTOR*, http://www.jstor.org/stable/30098928. Accessed 14 Dec. 2023.

Rosefeldt, Paul Nagim, "The Absent Father in Modern Drama." LSU Historical Dissertations and Theses. 5592, 1993. https://repository.lsu.edu/gradschool_disstheses/5592. Accessed 8 Mar. 2024.

Single, Lori Leathers. "Flying the Jolly Roger: Images of Escape and Selfhood in Tennessee Williams's The Glass Menagerie." *Tennessee Williams's The Glass Menagerie*, edited by Payal Nagpal, Worldview, 2016, pp. 185–205.

Van Laan, Thomas F. "'Shut Up!' 'Be Quiet!' 'Hush!' Talk and Its Suppression in Three Plays by Tennessee Williams." *Comparative Drama*, Vol. 22, No. 3, 1988, pp. 244–65. *JSTOR*, http://www.jstor.org/stable/41153361. Accessed 9 Mar. 2024.

Watts, Steven. *Self-Help Messiah: Dale Carnegie and Success in Modern America*. Other, 2013.

7 Conclusion

2024 marks the 80th year of the first production and performance of *The Glass Menagerie*, and my book *Essays on The Glass Menagerie: Truth in the Pleasant Disguise of Illusion* celebrates that. In 1944, Tennessee Williams was no more than a struggling playwright, though he had already written about six plays. His friend Audrey Wood gave the script of *The Glass Menagerie* to an independent actor, director, and producer, Eddie Dowling, who agreed to co-direct the play with Margo Jones. The nervous Williams decided to open it in Chicago first, instead of New York. The actors were not at all cordial during the rehearsals, and even as the premiere day approached, the situation seemed bizarre. They were having trouble memorising the lines and were faltering in regard to the correct accents. On 26 December 1944, just before the show, Laurette Taylor, the actress playing Amanda, was found re-dyeing a garment that she would wear in the play. However, as if by magic, everything changed the moment the curtains rose. The performances of both Taylor and Dowling turned out to be magnificent, as did those of the others. This is how the success story for *The Glass Menagerie* began. The next year, *The Glass Menagerie* opened on Broadway in the Playhouse Theatre on 31 March 1945 and ran for 563 performances until 29 June 1946. Robert Bray opines that Williams's dogged pursuit of fame got realised "by virtue of Williams's resilience, the play's superior material, the fine acting, and perhaps sheer fortune" (viii). Since 1945, the play has been performed constantly by community theatres and playhouses and major companies, and it continues to be one of the most frequently revived of all American plays. Here is an account of some of the revivals of *The Glass Menagerie* on Broadway:

- 4 May to 2 October 1965 at the Brooks Atkinson Theatre, Broadway.
- 18 December 1975 to 22 February 1976 at the Circle in the Square Theatre, Broadway.
- 1 December 1983 to 19 February 1984 at the Eugene O'Neill Theatre, Broadway.

DOI: 10.4324/9781003504245-8

- 15 November 1994 to 1 January 1995 at Criterion Center Stage Right, Broadway.
- 22 March to 3 July 2005 at the Ethel Barrymore Theatre, Broadway.
- 24 March to 13 June 2010 just off Broadway at the Roundabout Theatre Company.
- Previews on 5 September 2013 and shows from 26 September 2013 to 23 February 2014 at the Booth Theatre, Broadway, following an engagement at the American Repertory Theatre.
- 7 February to 21 May 2017 at the Belasco Theatre, Broadway.

As Delma Presley rightly says, the Broadway revivals in each decade provide directors "with new challenges of staging, lighting, and interpretation" (54), and actors and actresses measure their professional achievements by their roles in the play. Indeed, she adds, in the first production, the audience found the references to social events very topical and contemporary, and Dowling as Tom charmed the audience with his approachable manner. In 1956, when James Daly played Tom, he seemed down-to-earth and factual, and George Grizzard in 1965 was calm and understanding. In 1975, Rip Torn was a little aggressive, interspersing the narrations with accusing gestures and tones in a bid to make the audiences uncomfortable. In 1983, the handsome and blond Bruce Davison played a clean-cut and precise Tom dressed in colourful sweaters. Presley says:

> Tom of the 1950s reflects the placid Eisenhower years. In the 1960s it was Tom of the Age of Aquarius whose travels might well carry him eastward. The … 1970s, brought forth a defiant Tom battling against hypocrisy. In the 1980s Tom seemed more in tune with himself and reminded audiences of conflicts within the American family.
>
> (54)

Stephen Bottoms has documented the production history of the play since 2000 (68–72). In 2004, at the Kennedy Centre in Washington, D.C., Gregory Mosher's revival focussed on the social and economic realities. In 2005, David Leveaux's production appeared at the Ethel Barrymore Theatre, but New Yorkers as well as *The New York Times* found the production flawed and unappealing. In 2007, Rupert Goold's notable dreamy production appeared at the Apollo Theatre in London. In 2010, the Salisbury Playhouse team toured London, Oxford, Liverpool, and Glasgow and other major cities in the United Kingdom and, in an experimental bid, showed film footage of the young Amanda with her gentlemen callers. This was followed by the Young Vic Theatre, London production by Joe Hill-Gibbin. From 2009 to 2010, the Long Wharf Theatre Company produced the play in the Roundabout theatre, off Broadway, and the Mark Taper Forum Theatre in Los Angeles. Chicago's Steppenwolf Company took it up in 2012. *The Glass Menagerie* had a Broadway production again in 2013 at the Booth Theatre, a production that was also staged at Harvard University. Two-time Academy Award-winner Sally Field and two-time Tony Award-winner Joe Mantello starred in another Broadway production in 2017 at the Belasco Theatre directed by Tony Award-winner Sam Gold.

Even after eighty years, *The Glass Menagerie* continues to mesmerise audiences worldwide. Yet, as Harold Bloom and Robert Bray rightly point out, the general subject and themes of the play were neither original nor dynamic. As Bray mentions in his introduction to the play:

> It is no mere coincidence that many of our most memorable American plays, from *Long Day's Journey into Night*, through *Death of a Salesman* and *Who's Afraid of Virginia Woolf* up to *Buried Child*, depict familial tensions and alienations, the give-and-take of domestic warfare. Indeed, the venerable tradition of dramatizing family strife is by no means uniquely American, as this motif transcends cultures and predates Shakespeare's *Hamlet*, even going back to the drama of Aeschylus.
>
> (x)

Williams's young protagonist Tom Wingfield, like Hamlet, is caught in a dilemma; he wishes to be free, yet his ties with his family induce feelings of guilt in him. And yet, with a simple subject and theme, *The Glass Menagerie* has found lasting success. Interestingly, for the original production of the play, Williams recruited theatre composer Paul Bowles to write an original score that helped turn "a trivial little comedy of domestic tribulation" into the "legitimate magic" (quoted in Alfieri 143) and turned it into a masterpiece.

In a 1938 letter addressed to "All Directors, Actors, Designers, and Producers on the Federal Theatre Project," Hallie Flanagan, the project's director, wrote: "*The movies have beaten realism at its own game….* Just as architecture today stresses function, and emphasizes, rather than conceals, its materials, so the stage should stress the fact that it is a stage and should not be content to look like an imitation of a flat surface movie" (quoted in Alfieri 143). The same year, Mordecai Gorelik, stage designer, theatre expert, and historian, stated, "the stage, which once lent its technique to the cinema, is now learning valuable lessons from the cinema in return" (quoted in Alfieri 143–144). In the early 1930s and '40s, young playwrights and stage directors like Williams and Orson Welles began experimenting not just with light, colour, sound, body movements but also with new ideas and psychological analysis of humans and relationships. In *Hollywood's Tennessee: The Williams*

Films and Postwar America, R. Barton Palmer and Robert Bray mention that "[t]he complementary processes involved in moviemaking, especially the coordination of musical, lighting, and camera effects, fascinated Williams, who ... was to devote great attention to conceiving his plays as multilayered productions" (quoted in Alfieri 145). In fact, Williams himself stated that his play *Stairs to the Roof*, which came just before *The Glass Menagerie*, was written for both the stage and the screen, adding that some of the scenes needed to be presented in rapid succession very similar to the montage effect in cinema. As Bray rightly says, with the first great artistic success,

> Williams demonstrated how he could synthesize music, poetry, and visual effects into compelling emotional situations, structurally underpinning them with symbolic moments so arresting that theatergoers depart the aisles—and readers turn the last page—enriched with an assortment of moments guaranteed to haunt the receptive mind.
>
> (xv)

Williams's play began to attract the audience despite being a simple family drama because this family drama came encased in a new and innovative theatrical experience, a groundbreaking one. A new playwright had emerged who was fabulously blending expressionism with realism and surrealism in what he called 'sculptural drama' and 'plastic theatre.' It is for this reason that Esther M. Jackson calls Williams a pivotal figure,

> largely responsible for the development of an *American dramaturgy*: the art of writing, directing, acting and designing, a total theatrical form which is contemporary in its view of reality, American in its techniques of expression, and increasingly universal in its appeals.
>
> (9)

So universal is the appeal that there have been four movie adaptations and a television adaptation; and the play has been translated into several languages, including Bengali and Tamil (amongst other Indian languages), Brazilian Portuguese, Chinese, Japanese, Persian, French, Greek, Russian, and Spanish. *The Glass Menagerie* is based on certain ground realities that families face in diverse cultures. In the play, a middle-class family experiences tensions and frustrations emanating from a lack of economic resources. Low economic resources always act as hurdles for ambitious young family members and sometimes make their targets and dreams difficult or unattainable. All three members of this family-centric play are fractured individuals entrapped in their personal agonies. *The Glass Menagerie* has been celebrated universally, and it has transcended geographical borders and cultures. The answer to what makes the play still so popular with audiences is simple: the play has a human appeal.

Bibliography

References

Alfieri, Gabe C. "From 'Trivial Little Comedy' to 'Legitimate Magic': Music and the Making of *The Glass Menagerie*." *American Music*, Vol. 35, No. 2, 2017, pp. 143–71. *JSTOR*, https://doi.org/10.5406/americanmusic.35.2.0143. Accessed 10 Mar. 2024.

Bottoms, Stephen J. "The Glass Menagerie." *A Student Handbook to the Plays of Tennessee Williams*, edited by Katherine Weiss, Methuen Drama India-Bloomsbury, 2021, pp. 17–82.

Jackson, Esther M. "The Problem of form in the Drama of Tennessee Williams." *CLA Journal*, Vol. 4, No. 1, 1960, pp. 8–21. *JSTOR*, http://www.jstor.org/stable/44327928. Accessed 10 Mar. 2024.

Presley, Delma E. *The Glass Menagerie: An American Memory*. Twayne Publishers - G. K. Hall & Co, 1990.

Williams, Tennessee. *The Glass Menagerie*, edited and with an introduction by Robert Bray, New Directions, 1999.

Index

For Product Safety Concerns and Information please contact our EU representative GPSR@taylorandfrancis.com
Taylor & Francis Verlag GmbH, Kaufingerstraße 24, 80331 München, Germany

www.ingramcontent.com/pod-product-compliance
Lightning Source LLC
LaVergne TN
LVHW010939110826
845149LV00013B/2667
* 9 7 8 1 0 3 2 8 2 3 8 7 4 *